The Dirt She Ate

Pitt Poetry Series

Ed Ochester, Editor

The Dirt She Ate

Selected and New Poems

Minnie Bruce Pratt

University of Pittsburgh Press

The publication of this book is supported by a grant
from the Pennsylvania Council on the Arts.

Published by the University of Pittsburgh Press, Pittsburgh, Pa., 15260
Copyright © 2003, Minnie Bruce Pratt
Manufactured in the United States of America
Printed on acid-free paper
10 9 8 7 6 5 4 3 2 1

ISBN 0-8229-5826-0

Contents

Walking Back Up Depot Street, 1999

New Poems

The Dirt She Ate

Learning to Write

I am holding something too big in my hand,
a stick, a fat finger, six fingers instead of five.
My eyes trace, then my fist, the force that moves
down from the white letters on the blackboard,
to march   A   a   B   b   onto the page in front of me.

How I love that broad untouched expanse, how
it fades into distance when the letters spread their legs
and straddle its surface. Now the letters are mine,
yet they still sit above, staring down, elbows akimbo,
as we copy the morning's lesson: September 12, 1952.

Time divided into days, and my life into years
as I wrote. But what I loved first was the flecked blank
paper, the bound tablet like a book waiting to be
filled, like a basket, a bucket, a grocery bag.
The book of pages waiting to be turned,
an airplane propeller, an album of old photographs,
an empty field, unplowed ground, waiting for my hand.

The Sound of One Fork

1981

Cahaba

On the banks of the Cahaba
black walnuts are scattered
with their smooth skins split
down through convolutions
to the kernel fat within.

On the sands of the Cahaba
mussel shells have opened
their dull oval wings
and spread their opal,
pearl, and purple, skies shining.

On the road by the Cahaba
worn stones have shattered
at veins of crystal
where arrowheads lie
hidden but angled for flight.

In my town by the water
mothers, sisters, daughters
flow like the river
in the dry beds of men,
within crumbling limestone walls.

We could flood the fields,
spread the red mud to move
over house and porch,
split the sycamores through
to the white core of pith.

Our waves could break
at the surface and down

to the concave shell
to the vein of light
to the kernel of heat
to the arrowed flight.

Then we could raise
our eyes from the ground
and step where we please
on the banks of the Cahaba.

My Cousin Anne

My cousin Anne taught me
how to eat honeysuckle,
shook the dust from tangled vines,
guided my hand to the frilled petals.
She snapped each calyx
and pulled the stamen through
so I could tongue from it
the one drop of nectar
shining there.

We were girls when this happened,
when we leaned with our shoulders together
to quench our thirst with flowers
in the furnace of the summer.

We were still girls then.
Years had not burned between us.
We saw only each other
and the yellow honeysuckle.

My Mother Loves Women

My mother loves women.

She sent me gold and silver earrings for Valentine's.
She sent a dozen red roses to Ruby Lemley
when she was sick, and took her eight quarts
of purple-hull peas, shelled and ready to cook.
She walks every evening down our hill and around
with Eleanor Hallman. They pick up loose hubcaps
and talk about hysterectomies and cataracts.
At the slippery spots they go arm in arm.

She has three sisters, Lethean, Evie, and Ora Gilder.
When they aggravate her she wants to pinch
their habits off like potato bugs off the leaf.
But she meets them each weekend for cards and jokes
while months go by without her speaking to her brother
who plays dominoes at the machine shop with the men.
I don't think she's known a man except this brother
and my father who for twenty years has been waiting
for death in his rocking chair in front of the TV set.

During that time my mother was seeing women
every day at work in her office. She knit them
intricate afghans and told me proudly
Anne Fenton could not go to sleep without hers.

My mother loves women but she's afraid
to ask me about my life. She thinks
that I might love women too.

Elbows

Cover your arms.
Don't let your elbows
show.

That's what my neighbors
down in Alabama tell
their daughters
so no elbow
plump or thin
tan or pink
will entice others
to passion.

But if I thought
my scrawny, two-toned
elbows would lure you

if I thought
my skinny, sharp-boned
elbows could secure you

I'd flap my arms
like a chicken
like a peafowl
like a guinea hen

when next I saw you
honey
I'd roll
up my sleeves and
sin
sin
sin.

Romance

I used to drive down to the coast to sleep with her,
past the faded grey fields of sand and houses
closed up from the night. Sometimes there was a glow
in the east, like the papermill fires at Riegelwood. Then
I would curve where the land flattened to swamp
and the moon would flash orange, rise and turn
yellow as her hair, white and cool as her turned back.

All the way down, the moon shone through me.
I was clear as glass, ready to break under her look.
The moon shone down on my hands curled
tight around the steering wheel, shone down
into the ditch beside the road,
into the oiled water drifting there,
reflecting black light back into the stars,
poured down again into the throats of the pitcher plants,
onto the white spiking arms of the sedge, shone
down on the teeth and hinged open jaws
of the Venus fly trap, its oval leaves like eyelids
bristling with lashes, its leaves curved
together like clasped palms with fingers intertwined.

I wanted her hands to catch me and make me strange,
her green look to change me into someone else,
a woman who could move before her shadow did,
who always knew at first touch her next desire,
who was never the same from one minute to the next.

She kissed me with the mouth of every woman
who had kissed her. She gripped me with hands
and thighs as large as my mother's. When she lay

pressed against me, her breasts became mine until
I did not know who I was
                              until I began to wake
in the night turning between sandy sheets
to watch street light filter through the venetian blinds,
onto my hands stretched far from me in the phosphoral shadows,
onto her closed mouth and sleeping eyes,
the face of a woman I did not know, a stranger.

The Sound of One Fork

Through the window screen I can see an angle of grey roof
and the silence that spreads in the branches of the pecan tree
as the sun goes down. I am waiting for a lover. I am alone
in a solitude that vibrates like the cicada in hot midmorning,
that waits like the lobed sassafras leaf just before
its dark green turns into red, that waits
like the honeybee in the mouth of the purple lobelia.

While I wait, I can hear the random clink of one fork
against a plate. The woman next door is eating supper
alone. She is sixty, perhaps, and for many years
has eaten by herself the tomatoes, the corn
and okra that she grows in her backyard garden.
Her small metallic sound persists, as quiet almost
as the windless silence, persists like the steady
random click of a redbird cracking a few
more seeds before the sun gets too low.
She does not hurry, she does not linger.

Her younger neighbors think that she is lonely.
But I know what sufficiency she may possess.
I know what can be gathered from year to year,
gathered from what is near to hand, as I do
elderberries that bend in damp thickets by the road,
gathered and preserved, jars and jars shining
in rows of claret red, made at times with help,
a friend or a lover, but consumed long after,
long after they are gone and I sit
alone at the kitchen table.

And when I sit in the last heat of Sunday, afternoons
on the porch steps in the acid breath of the boxwoods,

I also know desolation. The week is over, the coming night
will not lift. I am exhausted from making each day.
My family, my children live in other states,
the women I love in other towns. I would rather be here
than with them in the old ways, but when all that's left
of the sunset is the red reflection underneath the clouds,
when I get up and come in to fix supper,
in the darkened kitchen I am often lonely for them.

In the morning and the evening we are by ourselves,
the woman next door and I. Still, we persist.
I open the drawer to get out the silverware.
She goes to her garden to pull weeds and pick
the crookneck squash that turn yellow with late summer.
I walk down to the pond in the morning to watch
and wait for the blue heron who comes at first light
to feed on minnows that swim through her shadow in the water.
She stays until the day grows so bright
that she cannot endure it and leaves with her hunger unsatisfied.
She bows her wings and slowly lifts into flight,
grey and slate blue against a paler sky.
I know she will come back. I see the light create
a russet curve of land on the farther bank,
where the wild rice bends heavy and ripe
under the first blackbirds. I know
she will come back. I see the light curve
in the fall and rise of her wing.

from The Segregated Heart

Nowadays I call no one place home.

For awhile it was a house on the highest land around,
a hill that lightning always struck during the summer
storms when I watched the sky go green and black
and suddenly begin to move. Then the trees belonged
less to the ground than to the upper air.
The oaks and hickories bent almost to break,
their leaves turned inside out by gusts of rain,
their branches whirling, vanished, reappeared
quick as the fire that leapt up in the distance
to shatter itself in branching veins of light,
then instantly be whole again. From within, I heard
the thunder, the clouds travel to the edge of hills.
I wanted to take their motion for my own and yet
I wanted to stay, to see the new leaves reflecting in the sun,
millions of green mirrors hanging from the trees.

Within the house, down the narrow hallway,
in the small rooms, we lived each day the same.
Politely and in silence we ate in the kitchen,
I took my napkin from the silver ring that bore my name,
my mother helped us to food while Laura who had cooked it
went to sit in a chair in another room.

Laura and I sat long afternoons without talking.
I could not understand her words, yet I heard
her breath rattle through the house to join the others,
the sudden noises made by those partitioned into sorrow,
the weeping of my mother late at night behind a door,
the rush of water she used to drown her bitter sound,

the weeping of my father, drunk at dawn by the window
when he saw the green edge of light on the top of the oaks,
the click of his chair as he rocked and cursed himself,
the sounds made by those who believed they had to stay
while their hearts broke in every room of the house.

Each noon we returned to our places in the kitchen.
For us change came from the outside and brought no good,
like the thunderstorms that swept down from Birmingham
or the elm blight that cleared town square of trees and left
the stone soldier standing guard alone over my father's fathers,
names written in marble honor on its weathered base.

There we used habit to contain, to outlast despair.
Even in the cemetery where my father's mother,
where my namesake lay, barbed wire ran between the graves,
dividing white folk from the black. It ran between
the women setting lilies on the one side, the women hoeing on the other,
a fence to separate one heap of bare red clay from another.

The radio says flooding in Mississippi and parts of Alabama.
Outside my door, the rain washes pollen in a yellow stream
off the porch and down the steps. The pines have been in bloom
for the last week, the wind moves through them in gusts
and becomes visible in sudden yellow clouds that lift from the trees.
Inside my house, my floors, my clothes, are thick with yellow dust.

Before the storm broke, I watched the bees investigate
the corners of my porch, the oval bell of my wind chimes,
looking for a home before their swarm. I know inside the hive
the virgin workers lie, with bent head and folded arm,
each sealed within her quiet cell until waked from larval sleep
by the dance and beating wings of her sisters. At first flight

each fears to leave behind the fixed prismatic form,
each soars and returns twenty times, hesitates at the void of space,
the indistinct brilliant mass of colors, the yellow and blue,
the wind that twists her to and from her course.

She shrinks at first from the infinite loneliness of light
but knows she can return to the translucent walls of honeycomb
where her sisters work and others wait to be born.

I live with no sister and have no daughter to name or raise.
I have no home except what I make for myself. Today it is
three rooms surrounded by rain where thunder cracks.
What I left I will not return to: yet I live in it every day.
The radio says mill workers in Wilson have brown lung,
their cells of pink flesh filled up with cotton dust.
The radio reports four women on foot from a dance,
shotgunned: they bled through small pellet wounds,
bright red holes in their dark skin and evening clothes.
The police deny the connections: two crosses
burned in town that night, white flames fixed at right angles.

If I stand in the doorway, the storm drowns out the radio.
I put my hands in the rain, louder than rushing blood,
colder than the tears of my anger or despair. My home is not safe
but dangerous with pain that aches like a cracked bone healing.
I refuse the divisions: yet always they break again.
I miss my mother and Laura who raised me. They still live
in the same and in different houses. I live here knowing
that the separation ends only when it is felt,
that the whole mends only when the fragments are held.
I long for a garden, a place to plant in daylilies, then sit
and watch them bloom each year, but I do not work for this.

Instead I take my plants in red clay pots out to catch the rain,
then set them inside where each leaf will focus the sun

like a burning green lens. I sit cross-legged on the porch
and turn my life outside in and out again, while in the pines
rain pierces the dark green needles with silver thread.
I mend the separation in my heart. I hold the heart's sorrow
and it blooms red, the courage to speak across distances,
the courage to act, like spiderlilies rising unexpected
every fall, in a deserted garden, along old foundations.

We Say We Love Each Other

1985

Sharing the Eye

1

We live between the county speedway and the interstate
in a brick house with azaleas that foam orange and
pink under our windows in the spring, with roses
that we mulch with pine straw in the summer.
A repairman who came thought we were sisters,
three daughters of a man he knew on Churchill Drive.
When we go out in the evening to walk around the block,
we look quite ordinary, young women in tennis shoes,
no bared teeth, no glaring eyes or protruding tongues.
But the neighbors think it's odd that we live alone.
They mean: without men. They think we're three weird women.

We walk until the weather changes. The purple blazing star
turns brown, the wind begins to rise. Then we come inside.
We sit apart from each other but not separate. We hear
the wind rush over our heads through the tops of the pines,
like the tide coming in: constant, inconstant waves, the ocean
rising and running a long way inland. The pines bend.
They twist, seaweed in the wind, stands of kelp in the waves.

Inside the wind, we talk or we don't. We take thought
from each other. We write our lives over in flimsy notebooks.
The lamp holds us in a round glance of light, the pages
yellow as quartz, our words written as if on unpolished stone.

2

Once there were three women who lived together
on a small island of rock above the aurora borealis
where waves of purple, red, and orange light

splashed against them with the constant sea spray,
glazing their dark skin until they toughened
to glitter with the iridescent chitin of dragonflies.
Their hair coiled and hissed and crept
in the wind that always blew around them.

These women saw whatever they looked at,
knew it as entirely as any granite pebble
that they picked up on their beach, passed
from hand to hand, considered and put aside.
Some terrified men began the rumor
their looks could kill, their unmasked faces were
ugly enough to turn men to stone,
their hair was undulant, unbound, monstrous.

The young man who set out to kill one
got directions from three grey women
with a single eye between them. The eye was sharp,
could see through stones and men, but the women
quarreled as they passed it from hand to hand
and the boy stole it until they told him the way.

He got his tools from three young women.
Flattered by his interest, with gleaming eyes
they gave him the power of invisible flight
and a woven, embroidered pouch
that could expand to hold a woman's head.

At the island he caught the three women asleep,
the wind and their hair sliding against the rock.
He killed one, cut her head off, stuffed it in his bag.
When he wanted to command complete attention,
he held her up, dangling, in his hand.

The power dimmed but did not fail from her sight.

3

At midnight the pines are unmoving in the air,
cold stillness around them, water in the ocean deeps.
In our house I wake up, yelling in my throat,
a woman by my bed, another at the door.

I tell them it's the same old fear: myself asleep,
the man with a knife shoving in the screen door,
my mouth open but no sound, my eyelids stretched wide,
my look useless, unable to stop what I see.

One woman says: *We heard you and we came.*
The other tells her dream:

She balances on a rocky slope at the crest of a hill,
sliding but staying up, above everything,
the wind blazing over her naked skin.

Men huddle at the bottom, discuss how to reach her,
but at the attempt each slips and falls
down the glittering side.
She balances on the crest of a shining hill,
at the top of a glassy, falling, but never falling, wave.
She laughs. She has never felt so strong.

For awhile the three of us sit quietly on my bed.
The thought comes to me with the click of a thrown pebble
heard in darkness: We can dream and yet wake and act.

4

Toward morning the sky is black as the abyss
where the squid swims, tentacles and arms twisting,

where she turns the water around her to luminous cloud
like the grey that soon will spread from the east.

Just before this hour a woman cries out and I wake,
to hear no intruder but a passionate motion: the other women
behind the closed door of their room. In terror I hear
them tangle together with twisting mouths. Open,
opening in the eye of orgasm, closed. They are finding out
truth or the lie. In terror I remember the weapon of sex,
my body worn as a grotesque mask, the clumsy betrayal,
and then sleep.

        The room is entirely dark, and smells of roses,
dried roses in the brass bowl. Tell the truth,
terror has not been all. There was the longed-for gulf,
skin writhing down to stone, eye of the vagina staring,
a woman's sharpened ecstatic face, a look like my own.

I lie awake in the silence. Far above, the stars toss
in brilliance, the phosphorescence of gulfstream currents.
I finger my tiny clitoral pebble and drift to an edge:
spiral of nebulae, funnel of water, collapsing walls
when spirit and matter go hissing together through the house.

In the north above the pines, a star dims and brightens,
unmasked in the cold morning: ancient repetitive guardian eye.

Sharp Glass

Shattered glass in the street at Maryland and 10th:
smashed sand glittering on a beach of black asphalt.

You can think of it so: or as bits of broken kaleidoscope,
or as crystals spilled from the white throat of a geode.

You can use metaphor to move the glass as far as possible
from the raised hands that threw the bottle

for their own reasons of amusement, or despair, or the desire
to make a cymbal crash in the ears of midnight sleepers.

Or you can use words like your needle, the probe curious
in tough heels, your bare feet having walked in risky places.

You can work to the surface the irritant, pain, the glass
sliver to blink in the light, sharp as a question.

Waulking Song: Two

Waulking tunes are sung by groups of Hebridean women as they work woolen cloth with their hands and feet to strengthen its weave. The women measure their task by the number of songs needed to complete the work, rather than by minutes or hours. Each waulking song has a narrative, which may be altered by the lead singer, as well as a unique refrain. The refrains below may have been sung by women at work as much as a thousand years ago.

I

É hó hì ura bhì,
Ho ro ho ì, ó ho ro ho.

At first she would not answer
when I asked what was wrong.

Then she told what had happened
that afternoon when she went in to work.

Ho ro ho ì, ó ho ro ho,
É hó hì ura bhì.

Later she gave me the shirt to mend,
a thin K-Mart cotton

with lines of yellow blue and red
running from grey to brighter plaid.

É hó hì ura bhì.
Ho ro ho ì, ó ho ro ho.

She had worn it the winter we met.
Under the lines I felt her heart beat.

Many times I had held her and felt
her heart beating beneath that thin cloth.

Ho ro ho ì, ó ho ro ho
É hó hì ura bhì.

2

Ì u ru rù bhi u o,
Hó í abh o.

In the summer haze she had gone to work.
The man with the knife stopped her.

He shoved her from door to straggling hedge.
He jerked at her shirt and ripped the seams.

Chalain éileadh ò hi o,
Ro ho leathag.

He cut the buttons off one by one.
He raped her and tried to cut her throat.

He tried to cut her throat. And he did.
The red of her blood crossed the plaid of her shirt.

Ì u ru rù bhi u o,
Hó í abh o.

He asked if she liked it.
When she would not say *Yes*,

he glinted the knife and he laughed.
He laughed and he left. She lay in the dust.

Got up. Found keys in her pocket,
went home to her trailer, took a bath.

She washed the shirt, put it away,
and looked to see what else was torn.

Chalain éileadh ò hi o,
Ro ho leathag.

3

O ho i o hì ò,
Hao ri o hù ò.

We swore his knife would not part us,
yet fear divided us with many blades.

She did not want me to touch her,
to feel semen and dirt on her skin.

If I moved quick she saw
the sun flash on the knife blade.

She wanted to know where
my hands were at all times.

When I slept with my arm around her,
she dreamed he had her pinned down

and woke night after night saying *No,*
night after night saying *No.*

She feared that I would not touch her,
would not touch, and that I would.

Hao ri o hù ò,
Ro ho i o hì ò.

I wanted the red mark to peel
off her throat like a band-aid

so she would be her self
without this pain: unscarred, unchanged.

Not a woman who could have been
dead behind a QuikStop store,

a line of ants running from her neck,
a woman her friends would not touch.

Ro ho i o hì ò,
O ho i o hì ò.

After three months we wanted her
over it, to be done with dying,

while she heard her rape each time
a rock cracked under feet behind her

as she crossed an empty parking lot.
I heard her death each time

a friend spoke the word *rape*
as matter-of-fact as the evening news.

O ho i o hì ò.
Hao ri o hù ò.

That winter, on weekends, when we shared a bed
we shared bad dreams. We twisted in sheets.

Some nights she heard her voice cry out
and woke herself, breath tearing her throat.

Some nights I felt her shake beside me,
caught in the hedge in December wind.

Before I touched her, I called her name
to wake her before his hand could reach.

We held hands as we talked in the dark.
The shirt lay folded, unmended, in my drawer.

Hao ri o hù ò.
Ro ho i o hì ò.

4

O ho ì ù ó,
Air fair all ill ó ho.

It has been three years. The shirt
was mended, not thrown away.

We rise at dawn to dress for work.
I touch her bare arm. She is alive.

Her heartbeats rush under my fingers.
Her flesh is solid, not crumbled to dust.

Air fair all ill ó ho,
Ro ho hao ri rì ó.

Under my hands, her shoulders spread
broad, an outcrop of limestone.

Under her skin, layers of muscle
from heft and lift, the weight of her work.

She has made herself strong, enough
to knock a man down, enough

to tell me one night what his hands
had done, the exact, secret wounds.

Ro ho hao ri rì ó,
O ho i ù ò.

I wanted my hands to be rain for her,
to wash away all hurt, the trace of blood.

I did what I could. I took out the shirt,
sewed the buttons back on, one by one.

Sewed over each seam, twice, by hand.
He would not ruin what we had made.

5

Hao ri o hù ó,
Ro ho i o hì ò.

When she got to work at five 'til 8
this morning, a woman named Millie was shot

in the parking lot as she left her car.
The man with the gun watched her blood

disappear into the asphalt. Her boss,
other women watched from a doorway.

At first she asked for help. The man
left to rape a woman in the next street.

In emergency she fought with nurses
who held her to the cart, said *Lie down*.

She said: *I know I'm dying. I want
to sit up.* And she did, before she died,

while they were saying: *Be quiet, you'll be better.*
She was a secretary, three months pregnant.

*Ro ho i o hì ò,
O ho i o hì ò.*

Do you want me to be quiet? You are tired
of the words *blood, rape, death*.

So am I. I had ended these lines
at the last refrain. But this morning I heard

about Millie. I remembered again your blood
in the dirt, your neck exposed to the knife.

I want to keep harm from you. I want
to clothe and protect you with my arms.

I look at my hands that held needle and thread.
We resist by whatever means we can.

At work your arm has thrust, your hand
has hefted two feet of steel pipe

over the counter at a man who threatened.
You say: *Next time I fight back even if I die.*

Your hands are not quiet, your voice is angry.
I love you because you have refused to die.

O ho i o hì ò,
Hao ri o hù ò.

This poem is for you, to pin to the mended shirt,
like the paper slip you find in a new pocket,

#49, but you know it's a woman,
all day folding sleeves around cardboard.

At work, almost dead on her feet,
she folds the plaid thin fabrics.

She thinks what her hands must do at home.
When she leaves the line, the machines are silent.

Her steps make a poem to the rhythm of her heart,
like a poem for you, to pin to the mended shirt.

Hao ri o hù ò,
Ro ho i o hì ò.

We Say We Love Each Other

You say: *The trouble is: we don't understand
each other.*
                    Your sounds have fascinated me
from the first, the way you laugh in your throat
like a saxophone. But last time the radio played
reedy brass, low sexy, I started crying. (Last time,
in the car alone, and jazz being played in a room
in a distant city).
                    Lately I understand this:
I want your voice, mysterious music of your body,
yet our words, gestures, are from different languages.

If we are sitting on the couch, eating oranges,
sweet acid, like lovemaking,
                              and the phone
rings in another room:
                        you answer, you murmur,
my stomach vibrates, deep drum flutter at your sound.

You come back. I do not ask *Who was it?*
To me, intrusion, a push into your room.
To you, removal, uncaring of closeness.

Then we are sitting on the couch, abrupt,
separate. The bitter orange rinds sit
in a neat pile on the round dish before us.

I am sitting in a place made for me
by women, generations, Scot, Irish, sitting
on a little bit of land, holding on,

survival on an island, isolation, a closed mouth
in their own kitchen, self-containment.

You are sitting in a place made for you
by women, generations, Jews in Spain, Holland,
Russia, the Pale, Poland, Romania, America,
the pogroms, no bit of land safe, none
to be owned as home, survival by asking, asking,
knowing where everyone was, enemy, family.

Later if we talk about this moment, we observe,
abstract. Even as I write, I make it distant.

But we are sitting on the couch: separate, not abstract.
History speaks like a voice through our bodies:
how often we do not know that it is this we do not
understand.
           Fascination with what we have not known:
Your hand gripping my chin, drawing me to your mouth.
My interest in a yellow gingko leaf, in veins in my palm,
my look up, the sudden kiss I give you.

What we fight bitterly: voices scraping against
demanding, selfish.
           Where is the future we spoke of
between us, stronger by difference?
               We sit on the couch
trying to understand each other, pointing to an object:
What did you mean?
           Lists, signs, paper with pictures,
paper with words, poems, photographs,
repeating, explaining, exasperation, anger.
                Asking:

What did you mean?

    The other says she loves: how believe
when her words, her gestures, are not the ones that speak
love to you?

    We sit on the couch. You rub my feet,
my heels are small oval drums. The radio plays
something we can't dance to. The room smells of oranges.
After a while, we say again we love each other.

Your Hand Opens Me

Flat on our backs on the floor, boards hard as packed clay:

I've wanted to make love with you outside, your ass
sunk into a curve of dirt, my fingers sunk in you
up to the knuckles and palm: your hips, my feet
thrashing the leaves like some unknown animal just
out of sight in the bushes.
                                        Not tonight: we are quiet,
behind a door, away from the cold, the other women.

Quiet, your hand opening, opening me, to the width
of light made by one candle, opening my thighs
clenched against the night, an eye pressed to the window,
someone who might look at my secret.
                                                    I need
your hand moving in me, unpredictable hot fingers:
my throat opens, my mouth closes on sounds,
high, stretched, squeals as the swifts fall
in the chimney, jostled from their night roosts, thumping
behind the bricks: like my heels on the floor.
                                                        Sometimes
I'm afraid: when we make love or I write like this:
my need for you: that you'll look at me from the outside,
through the blank window and think *how ridiculous:* a woman
with face opened to a throat, words nothing but
squeal and thump.
                            I have been afraid: you have held me:
tonight your right arm between me and the harsh dusty floor,
your left hand pressing me open, praising my secrets.

You have loved me: so I can come to you again
like this: my need for you naked as me,
flat on my back, thighs open, against the boards.

The Fact of the Garden

With this rain I am satisfied we will be together
in the spring. Seeds of water on my window glass,
transparent sprouts and rootlets. In your backyard
steady rain through the heavy dirt we dug in,
our shovels excavating some history of the tiny garden.

Our blades cut through the design of a previous digger:
rotting boards, rocks, earthworms big as young snakes;
a tarnished spoon, pink champagne foil from a party;
a palmful of blue feathers from a dead jay.

We dug and planted. We intend to have a history here
behind this rented house. Despite the owner there is a secret
between us and the ground. In the wet dirt, our fleshy bulbs
and the pink cloves of garlic are making nests of roots.
The fact of the garden has satisfied me all morning:
that we worked side by side, your name round
when I spoke it: that my fingers worked in the dirt like rain,
the ground like a made bed with its mulch of leaves,
orderly, full of possibilities, acts of love
not yet performed.
                    Now the water's slap on my window
has made me think of something else, suddenly,
what I don't want to, the way I wake up in the night,
think I've heard a gun shot.
                    The memory, news story
you told me a week ago: the farmers south,
far south, El Salvador, afraid to go into their fields.
What does their dirt look like? I don't know.
Instead I see that some thing is being planted:
U.S. soldiers watching as others bury a dead
hand, arm, head, torso.

                    To be afraid
to put your hand into the dirt. To be afraid to go
look at your ground: that it has been cut like skin,
will bulge out like cut muscle: that on a fair day
there will be subterranean thunder, then a loud, continuous
hiss of blood.
                    I wish I could see only the flowering
bulbs voluptuous in the spring.
                              But what is planted is
what comes. In the fall, plant stones: in the winter,
the ground gapes with stones like teeth.

I hold to the plan we thought of: small: full of
possibilities against despair:
                              us handing out
sheets of paper, thousands, the list of crimes:
sharp thin papers delving up something in people
in parking lots, shopping malls.
                              What will come of this?
Perhaps people to stand with us outside the buildings,
to say again: *Not in my name*. Words adamant as rock,
and actions, here, in the coldest months, before
soldiers move again in the fields to the south.

Reading Maps: Three

By the map, Point Lookout is almost an island in the bay,
land clenched between two river thighs, Patuxent, Potomac.

The road runs into what looks like ocean by its heave,
pause, and collapse. Rain spatters on the car roof,
an echo of radio clatter an hour ago: gunfire, machine
guns, U.S. soldiers landing in Grenada.

                                          To a woman
not here, known to me only from a distance, I say: *I'm sorry,*
I'm sorry:

                    and lean into thousand-miled grey water,
blank as an unfocused TV screen. What is happening there?
On her mother's island, the small place marked by her words
in the map of her stories: what inside the coral reef surf
or by the lime trees where dark women pause in sharp sun,
work in their hands, the children of their hands nearby,
as the assault begins, blades of air slung from helicopters.

Here a salty wind thrashes and whistles, no bullets.
Behind me, gulls hang and creak in the wind like old doors
shutting. A door slams behind me:

                                    Home, after school,
getting to be a grown girl, I iron the cotton sheets
into perfect blankness. No thump shakes Laura, dreaming
in the straight-backed chair, upright, eyes closed, dark-brown
face crumpled in an hour's rest from generations of children.

I look at her sideways, the woman hired to raise me.
She knew me before I knew myself. Which lines am I
in her face? I can't look her in the face: the mystery
of her living.

                    Now I can only guess at what memory opened
in her sleep. Perhaps she heard another door close:

A muffled thump. The oldest girl hides with the children,
tumbled in the clothes under the bed, clasping them
caught in the broken springs. The white man's patched
boot squeaks by. Her mother's pleading ends, broken.
By spring the farm is taken. They leave the sloping porch
and go.
        Not her story: another woman, year, South
Carolina, not Mississippi. Laura never told me. I am guessing
because today, on the island far south, there is the slam:

the foot, boot, kicks down a fragile door.
                      I saw her,
last, tied to a chair, kept from wandering where she pleased
down the anonymous nursing home hall, an old woman
in a knit cap, a struggle with hidden straps, an orange bedspread
in her room, chenille, no pictures, no photographs on the wall.
Her eyes, blank, then briefly sharp as thorns, catch me.
Her hands grip mine: old woody vines, vital, knotty.
In our past she binds me to her: I can no more deny
I am a child of hers.
          The world says it is not so,
but she says: *So bad, so bad. So good, so good. Mama,*
mama, mama. Her mouth fumbles. Is it her, her mother,
my mother, her children, me?
              But I know who I am,
even as I pry her winding tenacious fingers from my hand.

I am the one, flat on my back, the faces of dark women
leaning over, three women in green smocks, on duty, unknown,
as I lie mired in my own shit, urine, blood, salty pain.
With tender words they are not paid to utter, they instruct
how to shape and expel the secret: *Bear down, baby, bear*
down, bear down. Their hands grip both my hands,
the straps on my wrists. They guide me through chaos,
quagmire and thicket of my flesh. As I crack and sink,
their eyes far above, steady as birds in a shaking treetop,

continue to know and save me.

                             Done, delivered, I am
severed and forget them: servants in the night labor room.
Perhaps, off duty at dawn, they wash their hands of me:
an ignorant white yelling girl.

                             I'm sorry it's happening
again, I say to the wind, breath of my betrayed mothers.

They are elsewhere, shaping words, or clay into new pots,
or readying spirits in the dissolved clay of old bodies.
They pick up plates shattered when the door broke, pick
themselves up from the clean-swept dirt floor:

                                    while I stand
asking from their hands.

                         I am of their hands. I must do
with my own, out from this almost-island of sorrow.

                                   The waves sketch
lines in the narrow sand, a map of foam given and taken
by the water, pattern of nowhere to go.

                              I drive the way out:
black asphalt road past a stand of pines, wind-bent green
sails on land at tenuous anchor.

                          The rosin-tarred trunks
mark graves of men from another century's war, prisoners
who carved chessmen, or, in letters home to Alabama, craved
butter, red peppers, sage, onions, honey, sweet potatoes.

As they lay, midnight, no blanket but salt spray, the wind
whistling off the water to pin them to the ground: or lay,
daylight, dying, vomit, white skin putrid with smallpox:
did any feel the land swell under him, the sea journey,
midnight in the hold, dark skin rotted in excrement, land-
fall to live as captive beast? Did any confess the secret,
the fear he died for rather than say he was wrong?

                        No words
here, nothing carved on a pine trunk marker, nothing
except deaths named on a pale shaft of granite.
                        No grave
open like the ones being dug in Grenada, ready to speak,
split wombs of earth; no grave like that of my father,
him just closed with his secrets inside a mouth of red clay.

My blood his, my heart a small coffin-box given by him,
his voice muffled between my breasts. Is he saying *Mama?*
Is he crying *I'm sorry?* Does he mutter stories of bestial acts,
the white woman vanished into the swamp, black alligator-
men, and her white nape all bloody? Is he turning, restless,
under the look of men who shovel red dirt on the grave,
servant eyes that know more than him, black crow eyes
that see down to the bone?
                    I don't know what he knew
at the end. Years ago his voice was staccato as radio
propaganda: *We are waging a war against beasts of prey.*

Where can I lay down the weight of this sorrow? I've traveled
south, miles, looking, on bridges suspended like riddles
between green islands, through red mangrove, black mangrove,
root snakes on either side. I've dreamed of islands deep
in the great swamp's belly, safety where the land trembles
and earth fragments break free.
                    Some delicately balance,
matted with yellow lilies: by day, small floating countries:
by night, sinking in clouds of blue flame, will-o-the-wisps.

Others bloom and rot and grow substantial, clumps of maple,
tall leafy wings that catch the wind: these islands journey.
I could track one at night by rank sweet musk smell.
I could not be followed. By day and night, the patterns,

water and dirt, alter: the tangled passage snares
all memory.

           I would choose an island for me and my lover,
and lay myself down there, lightly, light-hearted, naked
in the place of no more crying, in warm burrows of grass,
coarse thickets, blankets. We would eat blackberries,
speckled marsh eggs, hoecake while the cornmeal lasted.
In the winter, a fringe of green in the ice, the inexplicable
pucker of water from an unknown source, a trickle of river
beginning, and our desire. And if terror in desire, ours,
and not another's.

           The alligator nothing but itself
sunk deep, the silver coin of its eye shining in the mud.
Its silent drift up like a log, its metal-trap teeth
snap at a heron's reedy leg, its soft grunt like a pig.

Ourselves, sheltered in dry grass, grunting a little
in sex, four breasts tumbling. No one's boot to poke us
and him say *Animals*.

           Toward sunset, shrill voices
from far away would come closer: shrieking, praying, whistling,
clicking, blackbirds and grackles, to knit and ravel patterns
in the air: women, escaped from locked-up or hiding,
and flying to roost. Now they fall from the sky, flash
of wings, hair, arms, into the rustling trees, all resting,
no door to lock, night in the swamp.

           We two would watch,
gathered safe, blue night pulled over us like a worn spread.

A dream, a place I've never come to, though I've traveled
miles. I've gone to the very end of land in the night,
one road only behind and before me, no guidance from the stars
staring down through ragged clouds, a million drifting
eyes looking up from the water.

           I've come to the coral island

where a woman lived, old enough to be my mother, but not mine.
At night I went to her door to ask for the secret: how to find
a place without sorrow.

                 In the morning humid light
I saw in the yard the little papaya with green breasts dangling.
In the house, a cluttered table, a pink hibiscus mouth,
a cracked cup still in use, books, a creased yellow
map of the island. I sat at the table ready for truth,
for directions. In her quavery voice, she told a story:

Once there was a man who wanted to live forever,
so he wrapped his heart up in a cloth, locked it in a box,
box slid into a chest, chest pushed into a closet,
door closed and locked. He lived on, his heart safe
(he thought) as a vireo whistling in a gumbo limbo tree
on an island in swamp water. But he couldn't hear his heart
beating, and forgot where he'd put it. He forgot to look.
His secret heart shriveled to a lump of dried red clay,
and he died.

                Later she told: The years her muscles clenched,
tight ropes of flesh, guarding her secret's escape.
Her daytime fear of stares like thrown rocks, and at night,
the bolted door, the dreams of surveillance, searchlights pushing
at the window, malignant faces as she touched her lover, hand
resting on the hip of the woman by her, curved earth horizon.

Finally, she cast the secret of her love into a pool of silence,
a listening circle of women. Released, dizzy, her body
flew open. She unlocked herself in a new place with the others.

Of the way there, she replied: *Tell me your piece of the truth.*

Today, now, no answer. The radio chatters gunfire.
Waves open and shut meaningless noisy mouths on the sand.
From the end of land, I drive the question, road curved

toward home, north, past the bony shaking pines, past
the sandy fields, tobacco sheds, irrigation ponds.

Past the swamps of the Patuxent, the place of the Piscataway
and the Nanticoke, of fugitives and runaway slaves. Their homes
built in the low places: corn patches, pigs, rockfish
in hand's reach, the children raised under no owner,
maple seeds into wings like green grasshoppers, summer
fevers, the messages, plans for rebellion and freeing the land,
the sudden bloody raids by armed white men, capture
or escape.
        By fall, the brief grass shelters overrun
with catbrier, bullbrier, wild grape, and the struggle begun
somewhere else: a river lowland, the Mobile, the Tombigbee,
or in the river of grass, Pahokee, Okeefenokee, or north
along the Combahee, the Lumbee, the Cape Fear, the Mattaponi,
the Potomac.
        I drive north toward that old swamp, the city
with monuments squatting huge as gravestones, its central dome
built with slave labor.
        I imagine snakes of kudzu
vines wrapping the marble office buildings, sarcophagi:
no one in or out, no devouring war, no mechanical
heartbeat of helicopters thudding over the beaches
of a small green island no wider than this capital city.

This afternoon, the numbness of repetition: despisal, attack,
theft of another's life, the boast of violence happening
again.
        But I have a long story I keep against despair:

Me and a girl friend, us not quite grown, in the abandoned
house, graffiti, forbidden red and black on the wall, the cold,
the rotten linoleum, us shivering as we clear a space to sit

in the empty room full of what could happen.
                                        In two years,
her flight, runaway from the small town, assembly line,
rest of her life in the factory squaring children's blocks,
or in a house crammed with children. The police find her,
crouched, fetal, behind an attic door, no money, no place to go.

I don't ask her what happened. *I give up on her*
were the words I wrote. We were alike, too close, she might
drag me down. I had plans for myself, I had a way to escape.

Twenty years later, she calls, she says: *I gave up*
on you. That spring when I was out walking, and saw
him open the car door for you. You got in, he closed the door,
you drove off with him. That was when I gave up on you.

Later she speaks of a woman on the ward who'd come
in with razor-marked skin, her sketch of life's bloody map.

She asks: *What will happen different, now?*

Later we talk of how we had danced: two girls,
the galloping staggering wheel of a polka, our thighs clearing
a wider and wider space on the cold slippery floor.

Crime Against Nature

1990

Poem for My Sons

When you were born, all the poets I knew
were men, dads eloquent on their sleeping
babes and the future: Coleridge at midnight,
Yeats' prayer that his daughter lack opinions,
his son be high and mighty, think and act.
You've read the new father's loud eloquence,
fiery sparks written in a silent house
breathing with the mother's exhausted sleep.

When you were born, my first, what I thought was
milk: my breasts sore, engorged, but not enough
when you woke. With you, my youngest, I did not
think: my head unraised for three days, mind-dead
from waist-down anesthetic labor, saddle
block, no walking either.
                                              Your father was then
the poet I'd ceased to be when I got married.
It's taken me years to write this to you.

I had to make a future, willful, voluble,
lascivious, a thinker, a long walker,
unstruck transgressor, furious, shouting,
voluptuous, a lover, a smeller of blood,
milk, a woman mean as she can be some nights,
existence I could pray to, capable of
poetry.
               Now here we are. You are men,
and I am not the woman who rocked you
in the sweet reek of penicillin, sour milk,
the girl who could not imagine herself
or a future more than a warm walled room,

had no words but the pap of the expected,
and so, those nights, could not wish for you.

But now I have spoken, my self, I can ask
for you: That you'll know evil when you smell it;
that you'll know good and do it, and see how both
run loose through your lives; that then you'll remember
you come from dirt and history; that you'll choose
memory, not anesthesia; that you'll have work
you love, hindering no one, a path crossing
at boundary markers where you question power;
that your loves will match you thought for thought
in the long heat of blood and fact of bone.

Words not so romantic nor so grandly tossed
as if I'd summoned the universe to be
at your disposal.
                    I can only pray:

That you'll never ask for the weather, earth,
angels, women, or other lives to obey you.

That you'll remember me, who crossed, recrossed
you,
        as a woman making slowly toward
an unknown place where you could be with me,
like a woman on foot, in a long stepping out.

Justice, Come Down

A huge sound waits, bound in the ice,
in the icicle roots, in the buds of snow
on fir branches, in the falling silence
of snow, glittering in the sun, brilliant
as a swarm of gnats, nothing but hovering
wings at midday. With the sun comes noise.
Tongues of ice break free, fall, shatter,
splinter, speak. If I could write the words.

Simple, like turning a page, to say *Write
what happened*, but this means a return
to the cold place where I am being punished.
Alone to the stony circle where I am frozen,
the empty space, children, mother, father gone,
lover gone away. There grief still sits
and waits, grim, numb, keeping company with
anger. I can smell my anger like sulfur-
struck matches. I wanted what had happened
to be a wall to burn, a window to smash.
At my fist the pieces would sparkle and fall.
All would be changed. I would not be alone.

Instead I have told my story over and over
at parties, on the edge of meetings, my life
clenched in my fist, my eyes brittle as glass.

Ashamed, people turned their faces away
from the woman ranting, asking: *Justice,
stretch out your hand. Come down, glittering,
from where you have hidden yourself away.*

Declared Not Fit

In this month of grief I am crying for my lover.
Suddenly my children appear under my closed eyelids
inside my grief, as if in a pitch-dark room,
vision: apparitions heavy with distance, absence.

I think: This is how you see your past just
before you die.
                My eyes were the rearview mirror
years ago. The boys were small and round, waving
good-bye. Their eyes were the young eyes of children
looking at their mother, that she will explain.

What were the reasons? Power of a man over
a woman, his children: his hand on power he lacked,
that my womb had made children as the eye makes a look.

What were the reasons? Terror of a man left alone,
the terror at a gesture: my hand sliding from her
soft pulse neck, to jawbone, chin, mouth met,
mouth of sharp salt. We walked the barrier island,
us, the two boys, the skittering orange crabs,
public deserted beach. In front of the children.

The danger: eyes taught not to cringe away,
the power of their eyes drawn to our joined hands.

Filthy, unfit, not to touch:
                those from my womb,
red birthslime, come by my cry of agony and pleasure.

Hands smeared often enough with their shit, vomit,
blackness of dirt and new blood, but water from my hands,
and in them, weight of their new bodies come back to rest.

When behind the closed eyelid of a door, in the heavy bed,
sweaty, salty, frantic and calling out sublimely
another woman's name, hands unclenched, I brought down
a cry of joy, then my mouth, mind, hands, became not fit
to touch.
              What are the reasons? I told them these.
They were young, they did not understand.

Nor do I. Words heard in the ear, hollow room.
The eye waits, sad, unsatisfied,
to embrace the particular loved shape.
Eyes, empty   hands, empty   waiting.

No Place

One night before I left I sat halfway down,
halfway up the stairs, as he reeled at the bottom,
shouting *Choose, choose.* Man or woman, her or him,
me or the children. There was no place to be
simultaneous, or in-between. Above, the boys slept
with nightlights as tiny consolations in the dark,
like the flowers of starry campion, edge of the water.

The month before I left, I dreamed we three waded
across a creek, muddy green, blood warm, quick cold.

    I warn the boys of danger, sharp drop-offs, currents,
    ledges like knives as we search the water with our feet.
    Like the creek at home, late summer, but the opposite
    stone wall is gone. We get across, footing sand
    on the other side. There is milkweed, purple-bronze
    wild hydrangea, and an unfamiliar huge openness.
    It is the place, promised, that has not yet been,
    the place where everything is changed, the place
    after the revolution, the revelation, the judgment.
    Groups of women pass by, talking, as if we are not
    there. Who can I ask for help? I am awkward,
    at a loss. We are together, we have come across.
    We have no place to go.

                We had no place to go.
I remember one visit, us traveling crammed
in my Volkswagen, no more room than a closet:
suitcases, model airplanes, an ice chest with food,
my typewriter, books, a bushy fern in a pot,
a spilled pack of cards, pillows and coats spread

in makeshift beds, the children asleep as I drove
past midnight trying to get to Mama's house
since he would not let them come sleep in mine.

How tired we got of traveling the night land;
how we crossed river after river in the dark,
the Reedy, the Oconee, the Cahaba, all unseen;
how night and the rivers flowed into a huge void
as if that was where we were going, no place at all.

Down the Little Cahaba

Soundless sun, the river. Home in August
we float down the Little Cahaba, the three of us,
rubber inner tubes, hot laps, in water so slow
we hear the rapids moving upstream toward us,
the whispers coming loud.
                               Then the river bends,
the standing water at the lip, hover, hover,
the moment before orgasm, before the head emerges,
then over suddenly, and sound rushing
back from my ears.
                        The youngest caught in the rapids:
half-grown, he hasn't lived with me in years,
yet his head submerged at a scrape of rock pushes
pain through me, a streak inside my thighs,
vagina to knee.
                    Swept to the outside curve,
the boys climb upstream to plunge down again.

I stand at the mud bank to pick up
shells, river mussels with iridescent inner skin,
with riverine scars from once-close flesh.

    Years back, at the beach, with piles of shells
    in our laps, with the first final separation on us,
    one asked: *How do we know you won't forget us?*

    I told them how they had moved in my womb: each
    distinct, the impatient older, the steady younger.
    I said: *I can never forget you. You moved inside me.*

I meant: *The sound of your blood crossed into mine.*

All the Women Caught in Flaring Light

Imagine a big room of women doing anything,
playing cards, having a meeting, the rattle
of paper or coffee cups or chairs pushed back,
the loud and quiet murmur of their voices,
women leaning their heads together. If we
leaned in at the door and I said, *Those women
are mothers*, you wouldn't be surprised, except
at me for pointing out the obvious fact.

Women *are* mothers, aren't they? So obvious.

Say we walked around to 8th or 11th Street
to drop in on a roomful of women, smiling, intense,
playing pool, the green baize like moss. One
lights another's cigarette, oblique glance.
Others dance by twos under twirling silver moons
that rain light down in glittering drops.
If I said in your ear, through metallic guitars,
These women are mothers, you wouldn't believe me,
would you? Not really, not even if you had come
to be one of the women in that room. You'd say:
Well, maybe, one or two, a few. It's what we say.

Here, we hardly call our children's names out loud.
We've lost them once, or fear we may. We're careful
what we say. In the clanging silence, pain falls
on our hearts, year in and out, like water cutting
a groove in stone, seeking a channel, a way out,
pain running like water through the glittering room.

2

I often think of a poem as a door that opens
into a room where I want to go. But to go in

here is to enter where my own suffering exists
as an almost unheard low note in the music,
amplified, almost unbearable, by the presence
of us all, reverberant pain, circular, endless,

which we speak of hardly at all, unless a woman
in the dim privacy tells me a story of her child
lost, now or twenty years ago, her words sliding
like a snapshot out of her billfold, faded outline
glanced at and away from, the story elliptic, oblique
to avoid the dangers of grief. The flashes of story
brilliant and grim as strobe lights in the dark,
the dance shown as grimace, head thrown back in pain.

Edie's hands, tendons tense as wire, spread, beseeched,
how she'd raised them, seven years, and now not even a visit,
Martha said she'd never see the baby again.
Her skinny brown arms folded against her flat breasts,
flat-assed in blue jeans, a dyke looking hard as a hammer:
And who would call her a mother?
                                        Or tall pale Connie,
rainbow skirts twirling, her sailing-away plans, islands,
women plaiting straw with shells: Who would have known
until the night, head down on my shoulder, she cried out
for her children shoved behind the father, shadows
who heard him curse her from the door, hell's fire
as she waited for them in the shriveled yard?

All the women caught in flaring light, glimpsed
in mystery: The red-lipped, red-fingertipped woman

who dances by, sparkling like fire, is she here on the sly,
four girls and a husband she'll never leave from fear?
The butch in black denim, elegant as ashes, her son
perhaps sent back, a winter of no heat, a woman's salary.
The quiet woman drinking gin, thinking of being sixteen,
the baby wrinkled as wet clothes, seen once, never again.

Loud music, hard to talk, and we're careful what we say.
A few words, some gesture of our hands, some bit of story
cryptic as the mark gleaming on our hands, the ink
tattoo, the sign that admits us to this room, iridescent
in certain kinds of light, then vanishing, invisible.

3

If suffering were no more than a song's refrain
played through four times with its sad lyric,
only half-heard in the noisy room, then done with,
I could write the poem I imagined: All the women
here see their lost children come into the dim room,
the lights brighten, we are in the happy ending,
no more hiding, we are ourselves and they are here
with us, a reconciliation, a commotion of voices.

I've seen it happen. I have stories from Carla,
Wanda. I have my own: the hammering at authority,
the years of driving round and round for a glimpse,
for anything, and finally the child, big, awkward,
comes with you, to walk somewhere arm in arm.

But things have been done to us that can never be
undone. The woman in the corner smiling at friends,
the one with black hair glinting white, remembers
the brown baby girl's weight relaxed into her lap.
The brown-eyed baby who flirted before she talked,

taken and sent away twenty years ago, no recourse.
If she stood in the door, the woman would not know her,
and the child would have no memory of the woman,
not of lying on her knees nor at her breast, leaving
a hidden mark, pain grooved and etched on the heart.

The woman's told her friends about the baby. They
keep forgetting. Her story drifts away like smoke,
like vague words in a song, a paper scrap in the water.
When they talk about mothers, they never think of her.

No easy ending to this pain. At midnight we go home
to silent houses, or perhaps to clamorous rooms full
of those who are now our family. Perhaps we sit alone,
heavy with the past, and there are tears running bitter
and steady as rain in the night. Mostly we just go on.

The Place Lost and Gone, the Place Found

One low yellow light, the back room a cave,
musty sleeping bags, us huddled on the floor.
We pretend we're camped somewhere with no calendar,
distant from morning when I will leave and leave
them motherless children again. The oldest travels
into sleep, holds my hand while I listen, left,
to a huge wind come up in my hollow ears, my breath,
pain, and me asking: What are we besides this pain,
this frail momentary clasp?
                              Next day at the window
the face of the youngest stiff with grief, and at my desk
beside me years after, his face, clear, fixed,
like a photo set in a paperweight, crystal heavy pain.
Pick it up, unable to put it down.
                              Yet woven,
still twined in my hand, his sinewy fingers like twigs
in the tree we climbed the first day:
                                    As soon as I jumped
from the car and hugged them, each a small *oomph*,
they rushed me to climb their tree, maple in the jumbled
wild green strip of land between houses and lawns,
up, feet here, there's the nest, rumpled,
suspended. They long for the hidden bird. We talk
about what I can't remember, nothing but words. We drop
seeds into light, translucent silent whirligigs.
Better than copters, they say, and gently rock
the branch I sit on with their long scratched legs.

They have asked me into their tree and, satisfied,
we sit rather large in its airy room. Their house

slides away across the lawn to the edge. Now
we are in the middle. Now they show me the inside:

If I see a small grass motion, it's probably voles.
That muddy excavation will be dug bigger, longer,
for a cave, for a hideout with a tin roof. And all
paths, distinct or vague in the rank weeds, go
places. The oldest boy leads me to his, a pond
sunk, hedged, and forgotten. No one else comes.
He watches in the morning (silver), in the evening (gold).
For what? For the birds, to be the one who sees
and takes the bird away, but only with his eyes.

The youngest boy takes me to the smallest creek.
We see the crawfish towers squiggled in the mud.
We see dim passageways down to hidden creatures,
mysteries. We follow scarce water under a road
into sun. They show me jewel-weed, touch-me-not,
dangling red-orange tiny ears, and the brown pods,
how seed rattles and springs and scatters if you fling
out your hand, even carelessly. They show me everything,
saying, with no words, they have thought of me here,
and here I am with them in the in-between places.

A Waving Hand

Last night of the visit, the youngest put his head
down, saying *Again and again and again and again
and again*, his head down on the bed.
                                        And I said
we should get a medal for every time we say good-bye,
like a purple heart, or we could have a waving hand.
(*Like the one in the windows of roaring trucks,*
he says.)
            Our chests would be heavy with
medals, heavy waving hands: pendulum:

We come back, we say hello. He cheered up, then.

from Shame

1

I ask for justice but do not release
myself. Do I think I was wrong? Yes.
Of course. Was wrong. Am wrong. Can
justify everything except their pain.
Even now their cries rattle in my ears
like icy winds pierce in cold weather.
Even now a tenderness from their cries.

The past repeats in fragments: What I
see is everybody watching, me included,
as a selfish woman leaves her children,
two small boys hardly more than babies.

Though I say he took them, and my theories
explain power, how he thought he'd force
me to choose, me or them, her or them.

2

How I wanted her slant humid body,
that first woman, silent reach.
How I began with her furtive mouth,
her silences, her hand fucking me
back of the van, beach sand grit
scritch at my jeans, low tide.

> The boys yelling in myrtle thickets
> outside, hurl pell-mell, count hide-
> and-seek. The youngest opens the door.

What I am doing is escape into clouds,
grey heat, promise of thunderstorm
not ominous, not sordid, from ground
to air, like us flying kites in March.
But to him it's July, and I'm doing what?

Curious, left out, he tells some fragment later
to the father, who already knows. The threats
get worse, spat curses: He'll take the children,
I can go fly where I damn please in the world.
The muttered words for scum, something rotten,
flies buzzing, futile, mean.
                              If I had been
more ashamed, if I had not wanted the world.
If I had hid my lust, I might not have lost
them. This is where the shame starts.

If I had not been so starved, if I had been
more ashamed and hid. No end to this blame.

3

At times I can say it was good, even better
for them, my hunger for her. Now that we're
here, they've grown up, survived, no suicides,
despite their talk of walks in front of cars,
smashing through plate glass. Despite guilt:

    The long sweating calls to the twelve-year-
    old, saying *Hold on* against the pain,
    how I knew it from when I left, the blame
    inside, the splintered self, saying to him *Walk
    out*, remind the body you are alive, even if
    rain is freezing in the thickets to clatter

like icy seeds, even if you are the only one
plodding through the drifts of grainy snow.

Now we've survived. They call to talk poetry
or chaos of physics. Out of the blue to hear
their voices, a kind of forgiveness, a giddy
lifting of my heart:
                  As they appear today in my city,
old enough to come by plane or train to be with me
and my lover, sit in my kitchen, snug, but a feeling of travel.
Their curious eyes on a life that widens in a place
little known, our pleasure without shame. We talk
and the walls seem to shift and expand around us.
The breaking of some frozen frame. The youngest jokes
lovebirds at our held hands. Late evening we stir.
Goodnight: They expect me to go off to bed with her.

5

In one hand, the memory of pain.
I read one of these poems and begin
again (again, it's been fifteen years)
to cry at the fragmented naked faces,
at the noise of the crying, somewhere
inside us, even now, like an old wind.
In one hand, the memory of pain.

In the other hand, change. When
did it begin? Over and over. Once
we all were walking on the street,
me and her, hand in hand, very loud,
singing sixties rock-and-roll, shake,
rattle, strolling, smiling, indecent

(but not quite illegal), escaped
out with the boys in a gusty wind.
The youngest sang, the oldest lagged,
ashamed? But we waited for him.
It was a comedy, a happy ending,
pleasure. We kept saying *Spring,*
it's spring, so the boys brought us
to their lake, its body-thick ice thinned
at the edge to broken glass splinters.
The new waves widened and glittered in the ice,
a delicate clinking like glass wind chimes.

And now, sometimes, one of them will say: *Remember*
the day we all went down to the lake? Remember
how we heard the sound of the last ice in the water?

The First Question

The first question is: *What do your children
think of you?* No interest in the kudzu-green
burial of the first house I lived in,

nor in the whiskey, the heat, or the people sweating
in church under huge rotate hands in the ceiling.
The question is never the Selma march, and me

breathing within thirty miles, or the sequence
of Dante, five poems, a husband, two children,
no poems, pregnancy and the concept of women's

liberation, or how the rain was slick and warm
on my mouth on her mouth, or why poetry returned.
And, yes, I give a different life's version

each time, but no matter what panorama veers
and recedes on the blackboard, white wall, behind me,
someone chooses my two boys to face me:

accusers, opponents, judges? Then I tell a joke,
and never tell of the long nights I choked
on my own questions.

                      And never tell anyone, only we

remember:
            The long drive home, live heat

changed at midnight speed to wind,
our mouths singing, drinking the humid
cool breath of trees, and yelling swift

blackness to come home with us, reckless
in the deep night, carrying everything with us,
all life and even death without a pause before us,

the sudden red-eyed possum, live eyes
dead, impossible but gone, our cries,
grief, and them questioning me, miles,

or perhaps this happened after the curve
we hurtled and the moon, huger than a world
directly in the road, moved our moves,

low orange eye, high hot-white when we got home.
They were nine and ten, one moment
out of years, except years after, the oldest

takes me up the stairs to show
his first painting, acrylic oil blue-
black sky barely edging around a moon.

Enormous memory   child mother moon   orange moon.

Motionless on the Dark Side of the Light

When I try to get back to my mother
at first I don't want to see the child
on her knees by the bed who is praying
against her hands, face and hands placed
flat and cool on the rough blue-and-white
woven bedspread that burns wet, hot, wet
after a while in the half-darkness. Light
slices by her from the cracked kitchen
door, voices fall through into her room.

Motionless on the dark side of the light,
she kneels and listens to her mother talk
to her father, her mother's voice slurred,
desperate, a voice she's never heard before.
His reeks of whiskey, pills, death. Reckless,
the mother threatens to kill herself too.
Is that what he wants? In the lighted room
one of them decides. All the child can do is pray.
Her knees hurt from the rug, nubby as gravel.
She prays her mother will not leave her.
She prays in the dark room rimmed with light.
She prays to someone there, but who is there?
Does she ask out loud? Does she ask, silent?

The white fluorescence by her slowly widens.
Her mother has come to ask why she is crying.
Her mother says she will stay, promises to live.

The child begins to pray nights by the window.
Some nights the moon opens its full mouth and
takes her   silently kneeling   inside   fearless.

My Life You Are Talking About

The ugliness, the stupid repetition
when I mention my children, or these poems,
or myself as mother. My anger when someone
tries to make my life into a copy of
an idea in her head, flat, paper-thin.

How can I make any of this into a poem?
What do I mean by *this*? For instance:

Me standing by the xerox machine, clack, slide, whish. Another
teacher, I've known her five years, asks what I've been writing,
lately,

and I say: *These poems about my children,*

holding up the pages. Her face blanks. I'd never seen that
happen, the expression, a blank face—vacant, emptied.

She says: *I didn't know you had children.*

So I say: *That's what these are about. Not many people know*
               I have children. They were taken away from me.

She says: *You're kidding.*

I say: *No, I'm not kidding. I lost my children because I'm*
           a lesbian.

She says: *But how could that happen to someone with a Ph.D.?*

I lean against a desk. I want to slap her with anger.

Instead,
I answer: *I'm a pervert, a deviant, low as someone on the street,*
            as a prostitute, a whore. I'm unnatural, queer. I'm a
            lesbian. I'm not fit to have children.

I didn't
explain: A woman who's loose with men is trash;
          a woman with a woman is to be punished.

I walk away, carrying off the poems,
useless words, black tracks on flimsy paper.
So much for the carryover of metaphor
and the cunning indirection of the poet (me)

who lures the listener (her) deeper and deeper
with bright images, through thorns, a thicket,
into a hidden openness (the place beyond the self:
see any of the preceding or following poems).

So much for the imagination. I don't say:
You've known for years who I am. Have you
never imagined what happened to me day
in and out, out in your damned straight world?

Why give her a poem to use to follow me
as I gather up the torn bits, a path made
of my own body, a trail to find
what has been lost, what has been taken,

when, if I stand in the room, breathing,
sweating a little, with a shaky voice,

blood-and-bones who tells what happened,
I get her disbelief? Or worse:

A baby-faced lesbian, her new baby snug in her closed arms,
smiles, matronizing, smug, and asks had I ever thought of having children?

Have you ever thought of having children?

What I thought as the pay-phone
doctor's voice pronounced jovial
stunning pregnancy, advised philosophy
(why he had five, this one's only my
second) was: Where would my life be
in this concept *mother-of-two?*
There was no one around to see.
I could cry all I wanted while
I sat down and got used to the idea.

At a friend's house for dinner, we talk about my boys, her
girl, the love affairs of others, how I like morning bed with
my lover. She complains how sex is hard to get with a three-
year-old around, glances at me as if to say: You have it so
easy. Does say:

Well, if you had children.

Other side of the door, the two boys,
half-grown, rest gangly in their sleep.
In bed, her hand slides, cold, doubtful
from my breast. She frets: *What are they
thinking?* While I whisper, hot, heat
in my breath, how I lost them for touch,

dangerous touch, and we would not believe
the mean knifing voice that says we lose
every love if we touch. We pull close,
belly to belly, kiss, push, push,
no thought in writhe against ache,
our sweaty skin like muddy ground
when we come back to being there in bed,
and to the sleeping presence of children.

In a classroom, we wind through ideas about women, power,
the loss of children, men and ownership, the loss of self,
the lesbian mother. They have heard me tell how it has been
for me. The woman to my left, within hand's reach, never
turns her face toward me. But speaks about me:

It's just not good for children to be in that kind of home.

I am stripped, naked, whipped.
Splintered by anger, wordless.
I want to break her, slash her.
My edged eyes avoid her face.

I say: *Why do you think this?*

I do not say: What have you lost? What have you ever
                          lost?

Later I say: *This is my life you are talking about.*

She says: *I didn't mean it personally.*

Over the phone, someone I've known for years asks what am I
   writing now?

I say: *I'm working hard on some poems about my
      children.*

She says: *Oh, how sweet. How sweet.*

I Am Ready to Tell All I Know

From the North (where cold white is falling
now) he says: *We are learning about the South,
in History. Terrible things have happened there.*

From the South (the edge, but roses are opening
their red mouths here, in November) I say:
Yes.

I am ready to tell more. I am ready to
tell him all I know. He says: *Let's don't
get into it now.*

He is fifteen. He says if he thinks about
it, he can't live every day: his math,
and rowing the red lake water at dawn.

I think of how I lost him as a child
when no one would speak for me
because I was *it.*

His tender neck lost to my mouth, and his brother
only a terrible absent weight in my arms, every day,
because my love inverted history.

I think about how terrible things
continue. At nineteen what did Michael
Donald think as they strangled him,

before he died in their rope noose,
hung from a small camphor tree,
black, in a cluttered empty lot in Mobile?

He fought them, he fought them.
The men returned to their card-playing friends,
soaked through clothes to white skin with blood.

When my children bleed, my own blood rushes
as if out of me. What if he were one of mine?
But which bloodied one, mine?

In the Waiting Room at the Draft Board

He called me the day after we invaded
Grenada. Low green hills exploded
into rock, flesh, people's bones.
I am ashamed of this country, he said.

Once he was a sack of living bones
I hauled. I pushed the heavy belly
uphill, months of summer and green war
in Vietnam. I sat down one afternoon,
lap full of silent weight. I sat
waiting on a narrow metal chair, cold
tin through thin cloth, my thighs
split, dull ache in my cunt. Waiting
for a uniformed man to come take a look:

> The father offers me as a piece of evidence.
> Clear to see: My flesh is the field, spread,
> plowed, and now the fruit, the root crop.
> Here is the land that needs its farmer.
> Here is the country that needs its ruler.
> Here is the child that needs its father.
> Let him stay at home and not go to war.

> I push my stomach out, weight drags
> my back. The man talks and stares at
> a thin swollen white girl, almost a mother,
> my belly cut by his eyes. Exactly what is
> there? Is it enough? Will it buy freedom?

2

Grown, he's asking questions about his father:
Was he an innocent man, victim, pushed
aside for my freedom? I retell what I've told
before: He was a man who escaped the war,
but when I left, he seized both children.

Maybe I don't mention the legal terror,
the threat letters: *Her unorthodox ideas*
about men and the father in the home. But
I'm clear about how the father was not god.
I'd seen his front, and his backside too.

I don't use these words exactly. I don't
throw rocks at his father. I tell stories
about how I fought him, some funny. We laugh,
lighter, as if stones have fallen out of us.
I don't know where he is bruised from when
I paid for my freedom with my children.

from At Fifteen, the Oldest Son Comes to Visit

1

There it is: the indelible mark, sketched
on his belly, tattoo of manhood, swirled line
of hair, soft animal pelt, archaic design,
navel to hidden groin. He squints, reaches
for a shirt, stretches in the tender morning
light high over me. My shock is his belly
like my young body, abdomen swollen pregnant
and luxuriant with hair, a thick line of fur,
navel to cunt. A secret message written on me
by him before his birth, faded, yet now surfaced
there with his body's heat, a physical thought,
a reply to my ideas about men and women.

2

A judgment on the father who took the boy away,
to find him night, day, sitting there, the child
who looks like me, goes up the stairs on legs
skinny and long with familiar muscles, the boy
who brushes at my willful brown cowlick peak of hair.

Now he's stretched out immense on my bed, reading.
I see a cleft chin, angled cheek, his father.

Oblivious, he shifts, muscles bulk, knot, vanish
in his shoulders. Since I left, he's shaped a self
stronger than his father. His call one night:
Trying to make me think like him. Last chance.

Soon I'll be too big. I say I know that wrestle,
that invisible bending, the mind's mark on the body.

   ▉

   5

He has my hands, wide palm, long fingers.
He has my big hands, which are my mother's.
Bit by bit our bodies gone on to our children,
like seed going to grass, long grass to seed.

Down by the river, the clumps of plume grass,
bearded grass in the setting sun, luminous,
delicate, hairy, taller than us this afternoon,
and my child taller than me by scant inches.

At a distance seen as man and woman, not son
and mother, walking, one of us at least wondering
how we might converge. The two of us talking
at the edge of a river flooded with warm rain,
yellow pollen foam, branches leafed-out green,
scraps of lumber splintered on the bridge: us

at this flux of violent water bound downstream.

Talking to Charlie

The cafeteria. Women, and alone, an eighteen-year-old
boy eating breakfast, diffident mouth, scant food. School.

I do not have to sit with him, not my child, but I do,
and eat my flat fried egg: cynical eye, yellow crocus
in the snow outside, speaking mouth. He opens
his mouth. The words will be: *Hate men, don't you?*
Last night he'd heard me read a poem: rape, the screw-
driver, the woman's eyes.
                                        His face convulses red,
muscles of his mouth struggle to push words fleshed
out, a new thing, onto the table between us. I gave
him something. He is giving me back a bloody live
making of his own.
                            He says: *The righteous anger of*
women The times I hate myself as a man. Not
to be. I get lonely.
                            His face. My sons look at me.

The three of us, faces bright as early suns, grinning,
reflected in the creek's surface, summer. We wade in,

swim, until four grim men arrive in the slipping light,
gauge with eyes how close we are until night, nod politely.

We leave. I rage, explaining. My oldest says: *If you*
hate them—men—you hate us.

                            At the table Charlie
waits for me to answer. *I get lonely*, I tell him.
What will you say to the other men? And to my sons?

The Laughing Place

There was the time I got mad and hired a detective,
I told the oldest boy one night he asked for more
stories. The cluttered supper table rattled and shook
like a car in low gear as he teetered back his chair:

It was spring after the fall I left your father,
and you, in the old brick house with the weedy yard.
He was after me, threats like boots and knives:
Sign the papers or *never see your children again.*
I was rabbit-scared foolish as if I'd slipped the pen
and, lolloping toward the bushes, heard the man's hands
about to snatch me by my hind legs up and skin me alive.

All spring I was in a sorry crouch, shank-shaking,
waiting. Maybe he'd get tired of whack, whack
at such stupid red-eyed game. I went and came
back for nervous visits, sprung free by the quick
tizzies of wind investigating the leaves that proved

summer. Then one day your brother, smooth-cheeked
innocent, crow-eyed, told me about the strange woman
sleeping cozy overnight like a plump feather pillow
in his father's bed. At first I was just aggravated,

and then, then, I got light-headed, hot-fingered mad at
this young Mr. Buck, laying down the law, do-as-I-say-
not-as-I-do two-faced deceitful man out to lambast
me for doing what I pleased, doing as he did but with a
different woman. That's how I got hissing mad as a cat

and called the detective up out of the yellow phone book
into the snack-bar red vinyl booth, a little slick-haired

weasel-worded gold-toothed man, *yes ma'm, no ma'm*,
in his lime polyester suit, green as slime, his promise
of a trail, a furtive gleam at the lit, lidded windows
of the house I later imagined him snoozing in front of,
easy in his rusty Chevy as a mole deep in his hole,
asleep in an earth of dirt, and not a speck of evidence,
mud or rock, to throw, nothing out of him for my money:

Except the idea of slinking in dark moonlight to pounce.

So that's what I did, with my lover, in her car. Sneaked
up the street to lurk and look for any pointed proof
I could use, mean as claws. We snouted, hooted, prowled
around the house, sniffed, flitted, plotted, but rooted
out only this: a bit of courage in my heart, canny,
cunning, that I could outsmart threat. Which I did.

I went to the hmmph-hmmphing lawyer and said *Listen,*
I have a story, told until he slowly picked the phone
up and called the man off me with *Careful, stones, stones,*
and people in glass houses. I'd thought I needed hard
evidence, a rock in the hand. I'd thought the house
was brick. I'd thought I did not know how to fight,
and all the years after, I've believed I did nothing
but tremble there for him to steal, kill, eat my life.

Now, telling you this, I've remembered: Those nights
I slipped around, playing the detective, making my escape.

Then the boy and I at the kitchen table both began to grin.

Another Question

Yes, they've seen these poems. The oldest says
nothing, yet. It's his voice I've answered
in them often, since the night he asked about me
and his father, *How did that happen?* I tell
the sorry story again, to him, a grown-up man:

> The words slide stone from the cave's mouth,
> and we enter together to ask and answer
> questions never voiced before. A chill,
> a crinkle of skin, as we advance into a place
> unknown, toward the oracle of ourselves.

2

The youngest son is debonair, modern,
reads Yeats, loves political words.

I pick him up from a summer job, midnight
in the steam heat of hot asphalt and the public
fountain. He's reading in the aqueous light,
gives me a dreamy traveling smile from a place
where he plots a clever footing of words.

One morning he reads my poems, serious,
and says he likes best what he remembers
being in (perhaps like this one). And also
that I get in the middle and tell it all,
grab people and tell them, just say it.

Yes, they've seen the poems. The world prefers
I not tell the children: hide, be oblique, be
secret, be grotesque. But the youngest says
when I tell it all, that's what he likes best.

Crime Against Nature

I

The upraised arm, fist clenched, ready to hit,
fist clenched and cocked, ready to throw a brick,
a rock, a Coke bottle. When you see this on TV,

robbers and cops, or people in some foreign alley,
is the rock in your hand? Do you shift and dodge?
Do you watch the story twitch in five kinds of color

while you eat Doritos, drink beer; the day's paper
sprawled at your feet, supplies bought at the 7-11
where no one bothered you? Or maybe he did. All

depends on what you look like, on if you can smile,
crawl, keep your mouth shut. Outside the store,
I, as usual, could not believe threat meant me, hated

by four men making up the story of their satiated
hot Saturday night and what they said at any woman
to emerge brash as a goddess from behind smoky glass,

how they won, if she would not bend her eyes or laugh,
by one thrusting question, broke her in half,
a bitch in heat, a devil with teeth for a cunt:

What's wrong with you, girl? The grin, gibe, chant.
What's the matter? (Split the concrete under her feet,
send her straight to hell, the prison pit fire,

blast her nasty self.) *You some kind of dyke?*

Sweating, damned if I'd give them the last say,
hissing into the mouth of the nearest face, *Yesss,*

hand jumped to car door, metal slam of escape
as he raised his hand, green bomb of a bottle,
I flinched, arm over my face, split-second

wait for the crash and shards of glass. His nod
instead, satisfied he'd frightened me back down
into whatever place I'd slid from. Laughter

quaked the other men. At me, a she-dog, queer
enough to talk? At him, tricked by a stone-face
drag woman stealing his punch line, astonished

as if a rock'd come to life in his hand and slashed
him? He dropped his hand, smiled like he'd won.
Slammed into the car, I drove away, mad, ashamed.

All night I seethed, helpless, the scene replayed,
slow-motion film, until I heard my *Yes*, and the dream
violence cracked with laughter. I was shaken out

    on the street where my voice reared up her snout,
    unlikely as a blacksnake racing from a drain, fire-
    spitting, whistling like a siren, one word, *Yes,*

    and the men, balanced between terror and surprise,
    laugh as the voice rolls like a hoopsnake, tail
    in her mouth, obscure spinning blur, quiet howl,

    a mouth like a conjuring trick, a black hole
    that swallows their story and turns it inside out.

For a split second we are all clenched, suspended:
upraised fist, approving hoots, my inverted ending.

2

The ones who fear me think they know who I am.
A devil's in me, or my brain's decayed by sickness.
In their hands, the hard shimmer of my life is dimmed.
I become a character to fit into their fictions,
someone predictable, tragic, disgusting, or pitiful.
If I'm not to burn, or crouch in some sort of cell,
at the very least I should not be let near children.

With strangers, even one with upraised fisted hand,
I blame this on too much church, or TV sci-fi, me cast
as mutant sexual rampage, Godzilla Satan, basilisk
eyes, scorching phosphorescent skin, a hiss of words
deadly if breathed in.
                            But what about my mother? Or
the man I lived with, years? How could they be so
certain I was bad and they were not? They knew me: girl
baby-fat and bloody from the womb, woman swollen-
stomached with two pregnancies. My next body shift:
Why did it shake them? Breasts full for no use but
a rush of pleasure, skin tightened, loosened, nipples,
genitals gleaming red with unshed blood.
                                            I left
certainty for body, place of mystery. They acted
as if I'd gone to stand naked in a dirty room, to spin
my skin completely off, turn and spin, come off skin,
until, under, loomed a thing, scaly sin, needle teeth
like poison knives, a monster in their lives who'd run
with the children in her mouth, like a snake steals
eggs.

I've never gotten used to being their evil,
the woman, the man, who held me naked, little and big.

No explanation except: the one who tells the tale
gets to name the monster. In my version, I walk
to where I want to live. They are there winding
time around them like graveclothes, rotten shrouds.
The living dead, winding me into a graveyard future.

Exaggeration, of course. In my anger I turn them
into a late-night horror show. I've left out how
I had no job for pay, he worked for rent and groceries,
my mother gave me her old car. But they abhorred me:

My inhuman shimmer, the crime of moving back and forth
between more than one self, more than one end to the story.

3

The hatred baffles me: individual, doctrinal, codified.
The way she pulled the statute book down like a novel

off the shelf, flipped to the index, her lacquer-red
lips glib around the words *crime against nature*, and yes,

he had some basis for threat. I've looked it up to read
the law since. Should I be glad he only took my children?

That year the punishment was: not less than five nor more
than sixty years. For my methods, indecent and unnatural,

of gratifying a depraved and perverted sexual instinct.
For even the slightest touching of lips or tongue or lips

to a woman's genitals. That means any delicate sip,
the tongue trail of saliva like an animal track quick

in the dew, a mysterious path toward the gates, little
and big (or *per anum* and *per os*), a pause at the riddle,

how tongue like a finger rolls grit into a jewel of flesh,
how finger is like tongue (another forbidden gesture),

and tongue like a snake (*bestial* is in the statute)
winding through salty walls, the labyrinth, curlicue,

the underground spring, rocks that sing, and the cave
with an oracle yelling at the bottom, certainly depraved.

All from the slightest touch of my lips which can
shift me and my lover as easily into a party on the lawn

sipping limeade, special recipe, sprawled silliness,
a little gnawing on the rind. The law when I read it

didn't mention teeth. I'm sure it will some day if
one of us gets caught with the other, nipping.

4

No one says *crime against nature* when a man
shotguns one or two or three or four or five
or more of his children, and usually his wife,
and maybe her visiting sister. But of the woman
who jumps twelve floors to her death, no I.D.
but a key around her neck, and in the apartment
her cold son in a back room, dead on a blanket:

Some are quick to say she was a fraud hiding
in a woman's body. Some pretend to be judicious
and give her as a reason why unmarried sluts
are not fit to raise children. But the truth is
we don't know what happened. Maybe she could not
imagine another ending because she was dirt poor,
alone, had tried everything. Or she was queer
and hated herself by her family's name: *crooked*.

Maybe she killed the child because she looked
into the future and saw her past. Or maybe
some man killed the boy and pushed her, splayed,
out the window, no one to grab, nothing to hide
but the key between her breasts, so we would find
the child and punish the killer. The iron key
warm, then cooling against her skin. Her memory,
the locked room. She left a clue. We don't know
her secret. She's not here to tell the story.

5

Last time we were together we went down to the river,
the boys and I, wading. In the rocks they saw a yellow-
striped snake, with a silver fish crossways in its mouth,
just one of the many beautiful terrors of nature,
how one thing can turn into another without warning.

When I open my mouth, some people hear snakes slide
out, whispering, to poison my sons' lives. Some fear
I'll turn them into queers, into women, a quick reverse
of uterine fate. There was only that bit of androgen,
that Y, the diversion that altered them from girls.

Some fear I've crossed over into capable power
and I'm taking my children with me. My body a snaky

rope, with its twirl, loop, spin, falling escape,
falling, altered, woman to man and back again, animal
to human: And what are the implications for the political
system of boy children who watch me like a magic
trick, like I have a key to the locked-room mystery?
(Will they lose all respect for national boundaries,
their father, science, or private property?)

In Joan's picture of that day, black, white, grey
gleaming, we three are clambered onto a fist of rock,
edge of the river. You can't see the signs that say
Danger No Wading, or the waterweeds, mud, ruck
of bleached shells from animal feasting, the slimy
trails of periwinkle snails. We are sweaty, smiling
in the sun, clinging to keep our balance, glinting
like silver fishes caught in the mouth of the moment.

6

I could have been mentally ill or committed
adultery, yet not been judged unfit. Or criminal
but feminine: prostitution, passing bad checks.
Or criminally unnatural with women, and escaped,
but only if I'd repented and pretended
like Susan S., who became a convincing fiction:

Rented a two-bedroom, poolside apartment, nice,
on Country Club Road, sang in the choir at Trinity,
got the kids into Scouts, arranged her job to walk
them to school in the morning, meet them at 3:00 p.m.,
a respected, well-dressed, professional woman
with several advanced degrees and correct answers
for the psychiatrist who would declare her *normal*,
in the ordinary sense of the word. No boyfriend
for cover, but her impersonation tricked the court.

In six months she got the children back: *custody*.
It's a prison term, isn't it? Someone being guarded.

I did none of that. In the end my children visit me
as I am. But I didn't write this story until now when
they are too old for either law or father to seize
or prevent from hearing my words, or from watching
as I advance in the scandalous ancient way of women:

Our assault on enemies, walking forward, skirts lifted,
to show the silent mouth, the terrible power, our secret.

Walking Back Up Depot Street

1999

Walking Back Up Depot Street

In Hollywood, California (she'd been told) women travel
on roller skates, pull a string of children, grinning, gaudy-
eyed as merry-go-round horses, brass-wheeled
under a blue canopy of sky.

                              Beatrice had never
lived in such a place. This morning, for instance, beside
Roxboro Road, she'd seen a woman with no feet wheel
her chair into fragile clumps of new grass. Her legs ended
at the ankle, old brown cypress knees. She furrowed herself
by hand through the ground. Cars passed. The sky stared down.
At the center of the world's blue eye, the woman stared back.

Years revolved, began to circle Beatrice like a ring of burning eyes.
They flared and smoked like the sawmill fires she walked past

        as a child, in the afternoon at 4 o'clock, she and a dark woman,
        past the cotton gin, onto the bridge above the railroad tracks.
        There they waited for wheels to rush like the wings of an iron angel,
        for the white man at the engine to blow the whistle. Beatrice had waited
        to stand in the tremble of power.

                            Thirty years later she saw
the scar, the woman who had walked beside her then, split,
but determined to live, raising mustard greens to get through
the winter. Whether she had, this spring, Beatrice did not know.
If she was sitting, knotted feet to the stove, if the coal had lasted,
if she cared for her company, pictures under table glass,
the eyes of children she had raised for others.

                                             If Beatrice went back
to visit at her house, sat unsteady in a chair in the smoky room,
they'd be divided by past belief, the town's parallel tracks,
people never to meet even in distance. They would be joined
by the memory of walking back up Depot Street.

                                        She could sit
and say: *I have changed, have tried to replace the iron heart*
with a heart of flesh.

                       But the woman whose hands had washed her,
had pulled a brush through her hair, whose hands had brought her maypops,
the green fruit and purple flowers, fierce eyes of living creatures—
What had she given her, that woman, anything, all these years?

Words would not remake the past. She could not make it
vanish like an old photograph thrown onto live coals.

If she meant to live in the present, she would have to work, do
without, send money, call home long distance about the heat.

Red String

At first she thought the lump in the road
was clay thrown up by a trucker's wheel.
Then Beatrice saw the mess of feathers:

Six or seven geese stood in the right-of-way, staring
at the blood, their black heads rigid above white throats.
Unmoved by passing wind or familiar violence, they fixed
their gaze on dead flesh and something more, a bird on the wing.

It whirled in a thicket of fog that grew up from fields plowed
and turned to winter. It joined other spirits exhaled before dawn,
creatures that once had crept or flapped or crawled over the land.

Beatrice had heard her mother tell of men who passed
as spirits. They hid in limestone caves by the river, hooded
themselves inside the curved wall, the glistening rock.
Then just at dark they appeared, as if they had the power
to split the earth open to release them. White-robed, faceless
horned heads, they advanced with torches over the water,
saying: *We are the ghosts of Shiloh and Bull Run fight!*

Neighbors who watched at the bridge knew each man by his voice
or limp or mended boots but said nothing, allowed the marchers
to pass on. Then they ran their skinny hounds to hunt other
lives down ravines, to save their skins another night from
the carrion beetles, spotted with red darker than blood,
who wait by the grave for the body's return to the earth.

Some years the men killed scores, treed them in the sweetgums.
Watched a man's face flicker in the purple-black leaves.
Then they burned the tree.

                            Smoke from their fires
still lay over the land where Beatrice traveled.

Out of this cloud the dead of the field spoke to her,
voices from the place where some voices never stop:

They took my boy down by Sucarnochee Creek.
He said, "Gentlemen, what have I done?"
They says, "Never mind what you have done.
We just want your damned heart." After they
killed him, I built up a little fire and laid out
by him all night until the neighbors came
in the morning. I was standing there when
they killed him, down by Sucarnochee Creek.

   I am a mighty brave woman, but I was getting
   scared the way they were treating me, throwing rocks
   on my house, coming in disguise. They come to my bed
   where I was laying, and whipped me. They dragged me
   out into the field so that the blood strung across
   the house, and the fence, and the cotton patch,
   in the road, and they ravished me. Then they went
   back into my house and ate the food on the stove.
   They have drove me from my home. It is over
   by DeSotoville, on the other side in Choctaw.

I had informed of persons whom I saw
dressing in Ku Klux disguise;
had named the parties. At the time

I was divorced from Dr. Randall
and had a school near Fredonia.
About one month before the election
some young men about the county
came in the nighttime; they said
I was not a decent woman; also
I was teaching radical politics.
They whipped me with hickory withes.
The gashes cut through my thin dress,
through the abdominal wall.
I was thrown into a ravine
in a helpless condition. The school
closed after my death.

From the fog above the bloody entrails of the bird, the dead flew toward Beatrice like the night crow whose one wing rests on the evening while the other dusts off the morning star. They gave her such a look:

Child, what have you been up to while we
were trying to keep body and soul together?

But never mind that now. Here's what you must do:

Tie a red flannel string around your waist.
Plant your roots when the moon is dark. Remember
your past, and ours. Always remember who you are.
Don't let those men fool you about the ways of life
even if blood must sign your name.

Eating Clay

Face damp on a lover's thigh and scratchy
pubic hair, she sighs in the wet dirt smell,
steam rising from hot ground and underbrush,
the hollow place, bottom of the hill, where
cars stopped for it seemed no reason, until
one day she saw a young thin woman digging up
the yellow-brown clay, crumbly as cornmeal
put in a paper sack. She'd never tried the dirt
but thought the woman had a power she did not,
tasting that mysterious meal late at night.

Now Beatrice envied no other's power, licking
acrid delicate salt from her lips. Not anymore,
as she lay back pliant in another's steady hand,
thou-art-the-potter-I-am-the-clay. Surrender.
Oh yes, the way she'd never done in church.

    Closest then she'd ever come was in the shed
    cool as a scooped-out cave, beside a dirt road
    miles from nowhere, in a world that went on with
    no help from her, even Ed could not do a thing
    when the wild turkey hen and her chicks crossed by
    but wish for his gun. The world went on around.
    Breathe, rot, eat and be eaten, regardless.

    In the shed, grey rows of pots dripped wet, just born,
    some small as a hand, some thick through the body.
    When the potter let her kick the board, the wheel spun
    heavy as a car on muddy ground, the squat clay lump
    sliding in her hand. The slightest touch changed
    everything. Thumb, hooked as if to peel an orange

at the navel, suddenly would plumb the earth's core.
Her fingers laid mountains low into glistening bowls.

Soon they'd breakfast off plates lifted whole from that place.
She'd set the table with a thump, ready for the morning news,
the next story about women like her, the same question:
What made you the way you are?

                                She'd say straight-faced it was
the dirt she ate.

                   And in the coming night she'd shiver.
In the candle's flame, the blue eye of a waiting kiln. Touch
scorches her breasts, her belly fattened with desire. The other
woman, panting, digs between her legs. Candle shadows
eat the wall, nether light swallows up the fire.

Sweat glazes her pale skin, done, undone by one touch
and terror, never knowing whether what will come will be
surrender, the tongue's flame in the furnace of the mouth.

The Remnant Shop

In and out the window the red silk curtain flutters,
breathes in with spring air, some hope of beginning again, out
with music, jazz, someone alive on the third floor. Not alone.
The bones of music dancing in the four walls of the blues.

She passes by the house and begins to plot. What costume, what
dress, what fabric, felted, knotted, braided, twisted,
intaglio printed, damask woven, what roving thread
would clothe her tonight? At the shop on Paterson Street she stops
to muss the remnants with her hand, whisking and tossing, silk
spilling through her fingers like water down a causeway, spill-
way. Three yards of silk tagged at thirty-nine fifty.

Thirteen dollars a yard, four dollars a foot, why she
didn't make that an hour when she worked at the plant. Her foot
stamped and stepped every two seconds, that's thirty times
a minute, and eighteen hundred times an hour and fourteen
thousand four hundred times a day. How many miles
a day? But you can't go far on just one foot. Hobbled.

She sat outside at noon, alone, with the other women.
They sat in the shadow of the picnic shelter. The white women.
The black women ate elsewhere. (Where?) So did the men,
the white men. No black men allowed. The white women sat
in the heat and said it was hotter than Shadrach's furnace. Hard to
breathe. Soon the inside of the plant seemed inviting, air-
conditioned. Like the icehouse. *Or the funeral home!* said someone.
No other cool place. The creek, spring fed, but you did that as a kid.

So she ate her sandwich in five minutes, and read the rest
of the half hour. She sat apart from the others, awkward, the book
open on her lap, the light glaring on the page as she read
Greek history. The names of the cities at war were beautiful
to her like no sound she'd heard except in the Bible, a sound
that opened a crack, a fracture, a fissure, in the parking lot
too hot to walk on, in the red dirt field, in the thick-walled
brick garment plant. She was going to slip through, if she could
keep reading and not hear what the women were saying.

> *The swollen belly. Ran away by the river. The church elders*
> *said don't never come back. The swollen belly. Everyone*
> *knew he used to teach her Sunday School. Everyone*
> *knew what she had done. Everyone knew. Everyone.*

Her head down, eyes on the page. The men with shields.
The red silk sails. The women at home weaving. Her head
down, and next summer the same, except on the line. Her hand
smoothed the fabric. This way, that way. Do the pieces match?
She touched the plush pile. She roughed the nap to see which way
was against the grain. She talked to no one about loneliness,
the machinery, people every day with hands like levers. Her foot
a lever that closed the circuit, weight pressed against
pure resistance, until an electric thread lock-stitched.
She held up dissected cloth and matched the halves and made
them whole. At the end of summer, she walked out of the silence
that rings when the buzzer sounds, and everyone switches off
her machine and leaves.

        In high school, economics was required
but she took music, and anyway no one would have taught her what

she's learned since, about the road from Ulaanbataar to Samarqand,
through Lyon and across the ocean.

The silk houses trembled
like water in the desert wind. The women hung their work
on mud walls, *ikat* eyes, red blue yellow, staring
into the sun.

In the Czar's plantations, fields of cotton lay
like snow blighting wheat and cabbages, while the peasants smashed
the sluice gates at the irrigation ditches.

On Croix-Rousse hill
austere buildings grew taller. Inside, the workers stood
in waterfalls of thread, jacquards overhead, weaving brocade.
They shouted: *Vivre en travaillant, mourir en combattant!*
struck the machines and poured through their hidden passageways.

She shakes out folds of fabric that snap like laundry in the wind,
skirts and pants on the fire escape, line out a tenement window
like where she lives now at the edge of palisaded rock, the fracture
where creeks and rivers drop down to a greater river, and the old
factories rise up as office buildings bright with flags
written over with new corporate logos, flapping in the breeze.

Where in 1913 the company sheriff tried to make
the strikers fly the U.S. flag when they marched. But they
refused. One held up his hand and said: *We dyed the thread,*
we spun the thread, we wove the cloth that made the flag.
We dyed the thread, with our very hands. This is my flag!

Holding up his red red hand, scorched sores, caustic eyes.

The sanguine curtains breathing in and out, imbued with meaning
by a human hand.

On her way home, every brick of the building
she stands in front of is clay baked and set in place
by someone who didn't own the land, the house, or maybe
even the trowel in his hand. The asphalt shingles on the roof—
someone pressed the felt, tarred and sprinkled it with sparkling
gravel someone broke from rock like that beneath her feet.
Someone set out the blue plastic pots, intending yellow
princess feathers. Unsealed the seeds someone had gathered
into packets.

Each person walking by is clothed in radiance
wrought by unseen hands, in the shoelaces knotted firmly
on the schoolchildren's feet, in the books they carry. Inside
are math problems and history lessons and poems made by
someone like her, standing on the street in morning rush hour.

Someone raised up by a woman told to keep the two of them
separate, never drink water from the same cup, the woman
who took Beatrice on her lap as the light faded, and held her
in the twilight, in the hard touch of her callused fingers.

The woman whose first job as a girl was to sew men's shirts.
She fastened on pearl buttons in a little factory down near Nanih Waya.

New Poems

Learning to Talk

On Magnolia Avenue there are no magnolias. Someone bought
the house of the one survivor. All morning I heard the chainsaw
sever its limbs from root to bud. No more scattered flowers, star city.
No pink galaxy. Now the yard is a parking space, one Jeep SUV,
one older car. Next door a woman comes out, late afternoon,
a child in her arms. She speaks low, as if there's just the two of them.
She says to him, *Listen to the little birdies*, and he listens to
the common sparrows talking in the hedge. He listens as they argue
back and forth, their dialect of nature, as the street clatters with commuters
taking a shortcut home. She says: *Listen*. And he turns his head to follow
the fugitive motion, the small streaked wings unfolding, folding,
the relentless chirp from a tiny blunt beak, the sound almost within reach.

Cutting Hair

She pays attention to the hair, not her fingers, and cuts herself
once or twice a day. Doesn't notice anymore, just if the blood
starts flowing. Says, *Excuse me*, to the customer and walks away
for a band-aid. Same spot on the middle finger over and over,
raised like a callus. Also the nicks where she snips between
her fingers, the torn webbing. Also spider veins on her legs now,
so ugly, though she sits in a chair for half of each cut, rolls around
from side to side. At night in the winter she sleeps in white
cotton gloves, neosporin on the cuts, vitamin E, then heavy
lotion. All night, for weeks, her white hands lie clothed like
those of a young girl going to her first party. Sleeping alone,
she opens and closes her long scissors and the hair falls under
her hands. It's a good living, kind of like an undertaker,
the people keep coming, and the hair, shoulder length, french
twist, braids. Someone has to cut it. At the end she whisks
and talcums my neck. Only then can I bend and see my hair,
how it covers the floor, curls and clippings of brown and silver,
how it shines like a field of scythed hay beneath her feet.

Doing Physical Therapy

In the office of torn and broken bodies, he flexes my foot like a rusty hinge.
Always polite, always the same questions, he listens instead to what is under
my skin: bones, nerves branching like lightning. He lays red and grey cable
on the poles of my ankle, then starts up the high-volt electric machine
to jumpstart me like a car with a dead battery. A light pulses, my toe twitches
in time to the shock: a picture-flash of a castle, a figure with upraised arms
beckoning the sky's fire down into a corpse on the laboratory table.

Later, I sit up while he instructs me to point my outstretched foot and draw
the alphabet, make the letters large as I can. I say I could write a whole book,
invisibly. He says, measuring my angles, *I know a boy with no hands*
who can make and eat a peanut butter and jelly sandwich with his feet.

Shoveling Sand

7 a.m., just light, and someone is already shoveling sand
at the construction site. A Black man leans forward, braced,
sneakers buried in the damp pile. He shifts to get his balance.
He knifes the blade in and pries up weight, straining for
a second, the pan low, like one arm of the scales of justice.
Then he flings the load up onto the screen sieve of the hopper
where it falls into finer grains. Mixed with cement and water,
mortared between rough blocks already three stories high, east
and north walls up, it will shelter the white men finishing inside.

Outside, he digs, and separates seashells, stones, from the sand.
The steady irregular beat of his shovel strikes like waves coming in,
high tide that crumbles and collapses a few inches of land, or as if
by the grave a hand gathers dirt from the edge and throws it in.

Day Off

Walking toward the clutch of drunks sitting in the sunshine
is like hearing a radio station come clear. The grumbling,
the accusations, *He stole from me!* The singing, one man
in a pure doo-wop solo, *One day, one day, one day.* Home-
less, their only work on Sundays is to remind us of shame.
The way earlier a man coming toward me crowded the fence,
averted his eyes while his hand wrung his mouth, the gesture
of one who is about to fail, the eyes down, remembering.
While tomorrow, on our workday, there will be the one who
holds out a paper cup at the subway, names the next train
so we don't have to run. After the door chimes shut, there will be
the man selling newspapers with his preacher's fear-god voice.
There will be the woman, singing, who steps the aisle between us,
past our averted eyes, shaking her collection cup like a tambourine.

Breakfast

Rush hour, and the short order cook lobs breakfast
sandwiches, silverfoil softballs, up and down the line.
We stand until someone says, *Yes?* The next person behind
breathes hungrily. The cashier's hands never stop. He shouts:
Where's my double double? We help. We eliminate all verbs.
The superfluous *want, need, give* they already know. Nothing's left
but *stay* or *go,* and a few things like *bread.* No one can stay long,
not even the stolid man in blue-hooded sweats, head down, eating,
his work boots powdered with cement dust like snow that never melts.

Reading the Classifieds

At the next table an African American woman bows her head
over a pile of newspapers, her hand slant to her mouth, then
to her ear, smoothing her temple, smoothing the pulse, fear.
Her fingers again to her forehead, then to her heartbeat hollow.
She sits, hair slightly askew, chin in hand, then quickly up and
out, a glance at the clock. Two days later, another woman, same
table, a Latina leaning forward into the paper, one hand with
a yellow marker, one hand at her forehead, a mirror gesture.
Her fingers pleating, smoothing, as her eyes scan down, over,
as her hand unseeing fumbles toward the brown lunch bag.
The other hand reaches to mark with a gleam the *data entry,
benefits*, the *experience a plus*, the *knowledge a must*.
Not yet the *no experience*, not yet the *home mailers, home
workers*, or *escort needed*. No faxes, no phone calls. She
gets up, bound for an overheated anteroom where she'll meet
herself, sitting on plastic stacking chairs, five, ten, twenty times
over. Next table a white man with shoes but no socks complains
about the cold, says, *This weather. This fucking
weather. Reminds me of what I was, on the street.*

Picking Up a Job Application

A spring wind hustles hundreds of pages into the street,
discarded leaflets like pieces of a shredded textbook
under the feet of high school students let out for lunch.
A young woman bends and grasps a flyer: sliver of promise,
passport to enter through the golden arches, gateway to the west,
up escalator to immediate opportunity, and prosperity somewhere
higher, those sky-reaching towers across the river looking down on her
and the crowd scrambling to buy a dollar forty-nine cent special meal.
Required? Just the have-a-good-day sticker on her backpack,
the smiley face plastered over her eyes and nose and mouth every day.
And one thing more, of course: *Fill in application on the reverse—*
English only please. She speaks Hindi, Arabic, Tagalog, Spanish,
Greek, half a dozen other tongues hide behind her smiles. The day
she says *Hello* to her first customer is the day she says *Hello*
to the other women behind the counter, who are talking, but not smiling.

Getting Money at the ATM

I can hear someone behind the money machine, a muffled
clanking. The screen blinks and promises me *any time,*
any where. A secret password gets me sixty dollars right
in the palm of my hand, dispensed quick as candy. And
not flimsy paper worn down like knee pads in work jeans,
but crisp new money fronted by old faces, by big men
who promise a pyramid of power, an all-seeing eye, every
thing is mine if I hold this magic skin mottled and blotched
with strange letters and numbers. Cash from last month's
paycheck, from electronic pulses, from the hidden vault.

From me sitting at my desk last month, phone to my ear,
words trembling on my tympanum, ten thousand words
pounding on the membrane, how many thousand clacking
between my teeth and tongue, the hyoid bone, the mandible
working without being named, how many thousand words
spoken by my fingers on the keyboard. Twelve eye muscles
twisting to follow the serpentine light of the screen. Feet
pushing the swivel chair back and forth, printer, phone, fax
machine. Taking a break means walking down four flights,
ten minutes up the street to the bank, then the post office.
At the counter I hand over money, a paper token, a one-page
book, all my comings and going hidden in it, mystified.

So, it's farewell and go, little book, and who will handle my life next,
and not know it? Then, it's back. Back up the stairs. Sit at my desk.

Playing the Lottery

At the table two women stare down at their cards,
classic bingo, cool cash: *For every dream there's a
jackpot.* The cards gleam silver pastel fire. On the table
are gloves, an old toboggan cap, two smashed paper
bags, an orange plastic pill bottle. One woman folds
her sandwich foil in half. The other scrapes her card
with a nickel, *Nada,* clicking the coin on the table
to clean it between boxes, as the numbers come up
silver and gold, each box a window, a hundred new
views. Or a door, behind each door a new car,
a luxury vacation, next month's rent. *No le tengo.*
Click, click, as if the turning wheel on *The Price Is
Right* is slowing down to reach its final destination,
after Vanna White dressed like a goddess has flung
out her hand to settle with fate. These women keep
their coats on, looking for something besides work,
table, tavern, bed, the chance of the numbers runner
who jogs past the corner, the casual lift of his hand
to grab the paper slip stuck high on the light pole.
One woman folds the scrap of foil again by four,
eight, sixteen, then drops it into her purse to save.
Every card needs just one more number to win.

Giving a Manicure

The woman across from me looks so familiar,
but when I turn, her look glances off. At the last
subway stop we rise. I know her, she gives manicures
at Vogue Nails. She has held my hands between hers
several times. She bows and smiles. There the women
wear white smocks like technicians, and plastic tags
with their Christian names. Susan. No, not Susan,
whose hair is cropped short, who is short and stocky.
This older lady does my hands while classical music,
often Mozart, plays. People passing by outside are
doubled in the wall mirror. Two of everyone walk
forward, backward, vanish at the edge of the shop.
Susan does pedicures, pumice on my heels as I sit
on the stainless-steel throne. She bends over, she
kneads my feet in the water like laundry. She pounds
my calves with her fists and her cupped palms slap
a working beat, *p'ansori* style. She talks to the others
without turning her head, a call in a language shouted
hoarse across fields where a swallow flew and flew
across the ocean, and then fetched back to Korea
a magic gourd seed, back to the farmer's empty house
where the seed flew from its beak to sprout a green vine.
When the farmer's wife cut open the ripe fruit, out spilled
seeds of gold. Choi Don Mee writes that some girls
in that country crush petals on their nails, at each tip
red flowers unfold. Yi Yon-ju writes that some women
there, as here, dream of blades, knives, a bowl of blood.

Picketing the Bargain Store, They Said:

We know the boss is out front getting photographed under
the red-white-and-blue Grand Sale banner, there
to remind shoppers of a national holiday, a victor's war.
We know we are inside fourteen hours a day, seven
days a week, once three days straight, no break,
one pizza each day to eat. Inside, we bend, grasp, lift
up onto the shelves the stuff for someone else's house,
bottles of bleach, welcome mats, thin pastel towels,
the green-and-gold peacock porcelain clocks,
each crowned head arched back to look at how well
it carries time in its belly. We make $2.74 an hour,
no benefits, no overtime. At night we sleep on the floor
of someone else's 99 Cent Dream Bargain Store,
and we are here today to tell you: *Basta! Not us, not any more.*

They said *Enough,* five of them. Not enough yet for the police
to unload the barricades and put them in front of the store.

Chopping Peppers

The slice across the top, at right angles, and
I am inside. If I did this for a job, where would I be?
Sitting on a milk crate in a restaurant kitchen. Who
would I be? Someone chopping green peppers for
sweet-and-sour chicken. I hold the slippery bowl
and inside is the secret, an island of seeds, a palisade,
a reef, an outcropping of the future waiting for decay,
for the collapse of walls, for escape. Instead, I filigree
the flesh into odd bits of ribbon with the little paring knife,
the gesture effortless, no more than a minute, time to play
with these words, and my fingers and wrist don't feel a thing.

I was no metaphor when I fed a machine eight hours a day.
I was what came before words, my hands the spring,
setting metal jaws to shut, the same synapses to snap
together every second all day again and again
until what is being done can be named.

Author's Note and Acknowledgments

For this book, I have revised many of the previously published poems. I have altered them to deal with infelicities, repetitions, or content that I now see strayed from the original path.

Because these poems were written over a period of more than twenty years, both they and I were shaped and helped by many people. My grateful thanks were made to many of you in previous volumes—and I thank you again for what I learned from you, without which this work could not have been done.

Here I would like to acknowledge those who have particularly aided me with these selected poems.

My deepest gratitude to:

Judith Arcana, Elly Bulkin, Nanette Gartrell, Jewelle Gomez, Holly Hughes, Joan Larkin, and Michael Lassell, for their support of my work over many years, for their detailed reading and helpful comments on this manuscript, and for their friendship.

Ed Ochester, inimitable poet-editor, for his continued commitment to my work; and the staff at the University of Pittsburgh Press, whose collective efforts gave a larger life to these poems.

The National Writers Union and Ellis Guzman, for help in negotiating the legal and technical vicissitudes of my writer's work.

My sons Ransom Weaver and Ben Weaver, my friends Dee Mosbacher and Rebeca Toledo, and my Saturday home group, for their loving support.

Leslie Feinberg, for encouraging me to do this collection, for insightful editorial comments at all of its stages, and, most of all, for your tender, challenging love.

The selected poems in this volume originally appeared in *The Sound of One Fork* (Night Heron Press, 1981), *We Say We Love Each Other* (Spinsters Ink/ Aunt Lute, 1985 and Firebrand Books, 1992), *Crime Against Nature* (Firebrand Books, 1990), and *Walking Back Up Depot Street* (University of Pittsburgh Press, 1999). Some of the new poems have appeared in earlier versions in the following publications: "Cutting Hair" and "Picking Up a Job Application" in *Ploughshares*, and "Doing Physical Therapy," "Learning to Talk," and "Learning to Write" in *Smartish Pace*.

Minnie Bruce Pratt is the author of four books of poetry, including *Walking Back Up Depot Street*, named the 1999 *ForeWord* Best Lesbian/Gay Book of the Year, and *Crime Against Nature*, chosen as the 1989 Lamont Poetry Selection by the Academy of American Poets and the 1991 American Library Association Gay and Lesbian Book Award for Literature. She has also authored a book of autobiographical and political essays, *Rebellion: Essays 1980–1991*; a book of prose stories about gender boundary crossing, *S/HE;* and has coauthored *Yours in Struggle: Three Feminist Perspectives on Anti-Semitism and Racism* with Elly Bulkin and Barbara Smith. An activist against racism and imperialism, and for social justice, Pratt teaches women's studies, lesbian/gay/bisexual/transgender studies, and creative writing as a member of the graduate faculty of the Union Institute and University. Her Web site is *www.mbpratt.org.*